EMBATS

IN SPANISH

and how to avoid them

**A Practical, Entertaining Guide
to Using Spanish Correctly**

JAMES N. MOSÉL

UNGAR / NEW YORK

1987

The Ungar Publishing Company
370 Lexington Avenue
New York, NY 10017

Tenth Printing 1987

Printed in the United States of America

Library of Congress Cataloging-in-Publication Data

Mosél, James N.
Embarassing moments in Spanish and how to avoid them.
1. Spanish language—Errors of usage.   I. Title.
PC4460.M69 1987   468   87-5919
ISBN 0-8044-6522-3 (pbk.)

To Kyra and Elaine,

who will soon be learning this,

the most beautiful of tongues.

CONTENTS

PREFACE

THIS BOOK is the outgrowth of several studies made by the author on the errors of Spanish-speaking Americans. The data were derived from teaching and the systematic observation of the Spanish of American students. The results of these surveys indicate that the most elusive difficulty is not one of grammar, but of usage. The cure for grammatical ills is study and practice, for which there are an abundant number of adequate texts. In the matter of usage, however, the problem is further complicated by the lack of any materials which might serve as a systematic guide. It is believed that an original feature of this small book is that it meets the student on his own ground and approaches usage from the point where he might take his first false step. It is hoped that in spite of its numerous inadequacies, this book will make an attractive initial contribution to the solution of the student's difficulties.

Usages are indicated according to those accepted by the 1936 edition of the Spanish Academy Dictionary. The Spanish American equivalents have been drawn from my own personal experience, but many of them will also be found in F. J. Santamaría's *Diccionario General de Americanismos* (Mexico City, 1943).

I wish to express my deep gratitude to Mr. Francis James Donahue, *ante bellum* of the University of Wisconsin, for his valuable criticism in the preparation of the manuscript; to the Latin American Institute, Washington, D. C., for the many observations made while teaching there, and to Dr. Manuel de Sainz of Cuba, one of the Institute's directors, for his advice on certain stylistic matters. I also wish to express my indebtedness to my friend and teacher, Dr. Graydon S. De Land, Head of the Romance Language Department of Denison University, since it was from my early studies under him that I first acquired the approach to usage which I have attempted to present in this book. None of the above, however, is responsible for the shortcomings of the book; they are entirely my own.

J. N. M.
Washington, D. C.
1945

A WORD TO THE WISE

"A buen entendedor pocas palabras . . ."

THIS LITTLE BOOK is to help improve your Spanish. If you use it well, it will assist you in avoiding those common and often embarrassing errors which have earned Americans the unwarranted reputation of "bad linguists." Spanish is not as easy as is popularly thought, for it contains many subtleties and pitfalls in usage which are a ready source of "embarrassing moments." Each item in this book has been carefully selected because of its importance, and therefore deserves your close attention. Many of these items are not otherwise accessible to the practical student, and sometimes many years of study pass before the proper insight is developed. It is amazing to note that many of these errors persist even after relative fluency has been gained. It is unnecessary to add that fluency does not compensate for the bad impressions and misunderstandings incurred by incorrect usage. The material of this book should therefore prove of practical value for both the beginning and the advanced student.

One of the main difficulties in the acquisition of good usage lies in the unfortunate fact that the dictionary does not indicate prevailing preferences and neglects the implications of the words defined. A very reputable dictionary, to cite one example, would have us believe that the prime meaning of *entretener* is "to amuse", "to entertain", and completely neglects the most frequent meanings "to maintain" and "to divert one's attention". It would be absurd, for instance, to translate *entretener una fuerza aérea* as "entertain an air force". It must also be kept in mind that the dictionary offers many words and definitions which are not a part of current usage. Dictionaries aim at being inclusive, not discriminative. It is also well to bear in mind that natives cannot always be relied upon in such matters, for in many cases their English contains the reverse faults. It has been the writer's observation that native speakers are often the last to appreciate the student's difficulties, for natives speak the language automatically and without awareness of idioms as such. The English-speaking student, however, must be guided by admonitions and principles until he has reached the stage at which he can speak correctly from habit.

In speaking, writing and translating Spanish, the most frequent errors in usage appear to be of three varieties: (1) attributing to Spanish words the meanings of their English cognates, (2) disregarding certain distinctions in Spanish which are unknown to English, and (3) translating literally without regard for the unique functions of certain Spanish words. This book has accordingly been arranged in three parts. Elementary students will probably find that Parts I and III have the most immediate importance, while more advanced students are likely to be especially interested in Part II. An additional feature, and one which is often neglected, is that Spanish American variations are given whenever relevant.

The writer also feels duty-bound to warn against another source of severe consequence which lies in wait for the unsuspecting student, and that is the *doble sentido* or "double meaning". In some situations, certain very common words acquire an entirely different meaning, a meaning which is often obnoxious and socially *tabu*. This is especially perplexing in Spanish America where usage varies from country to country. In general, however, you will spare yourself many an unpleasant moment if you guard against the following:

First, you are strongly advised never to use the word *coger* (get, catch, grasp) in regard to persons. In Argentina and Chile, the "other meaning" has become the predominant one, and the verbs *agarrar*, *pillar*, or *recoger* must be used instead. The same applies to *tirar* (to throw, hurl), which in some places (Colombia, etc.) must be replaced by *arrojar*. You should also avoid the words *caliente*[1] and *hembra* in speaking of persons, for these too have acquired additional meanings. In Mexico it is advisable to use *blanquillos* instead of *huevos* (eggs), and in Cuba by all means say *fruta bomba* and not *papaya!* Similarly, *cuernos* (horns) is seldom heard in polite society for its secondary meaning might be offensive; use *astas* instead. The words *sujeto* and *individuo* mean "fellow" in most places, but in Argentina their application is insulting. Note also that *señorito* does not have the same meaning in Spanish America as it does in Spain. In Spain *señorito* is a respectful title for addressing young boys (Cf. "master" as in Master Johnny). In Spanish America, however, it usually means a "Little Lord Fauntleroy" and is anything but complimentary for the average boy, Spanish American or otherwise.

You should beware of all dubious expletives and vituperatives beginning with the suspicious combination of letters *ca–*. Such words as *caramba*, *caray*, *caracoles* and *cáspita* are mild and harmless, but are substitutes for a series of more

---

[1] If you do not want Spanish girls to run from you, never say *estoy caliente* for "I am hot". The proper expression is *tengo calor*.

obnoxious and vulgar words. You should judiciously question any words which might possibly fall into the latter category.

There are many diminutives and augmentatives which are especially common in the colloquial language. Some of these have meanings which are too subtle to be safely employed by foreigners, and they should be used with the greatest caution. It is generally safe to employ *–ito*, *–cito*, and perhaps *–ecito*, but you will do well to avoid the others until you have become familiar with their use. In some situations to disregard this is to invite actual physical danger.[1]

One thing more. The Spanish mind is somewhat perceptive of "double meanings" and other plays on words. Thus you sometimes may find that some of your seemingly innocuous word combinations unintentionally provide a source of *chistes* and risqué amusement. Only after long experience with the spoken language can the student be expected to understand these, but a word of warning should at least prevent any resentful misunderstandings. You should remember that it is all *de burlas*, and that no harm is intended. The best procedure is to pass off the whole affair with some light philosophic remark such as: *¡Sí que metí la pata!* (I surely put my foot in it!) Then and there you will cease to be the *gringo* and begin to acquire the much coveted title of *simpático*. *¡Que tenga mucha suerte!*

---

[1] As an example, note the change of meaning in *mujerzuela* = prostitute.

I. BEWARE OF APPEARANCES!

DECEPTIVE COGNATES

MANY SPANISH WORDS appear very similar to certain words in English. In some cases the meanings are the same in both languages. and such cognate words provide an excellent way of building a vocabulary. On the other hand, it often happens that the Spanish word has a meaning quite removed from that of the English. The practice of indiscriminately attributing to Spanish words the meaning of their English cognates is a hazardous one. The following are among the most common of this type of error:

ACTUAL. This does not mean "actual", but "present": *mi trabajo actual* = my present work. The same applies to *actualidad* and *actualmente*, which mean "present time" and "at the present time" respectively. Thus: *actualmente* (or *en la actualidad*) *él está en la Habana* = at the present time he is in Havana. Express the idea of English "actual" by *verdadero, real* or *efectivo*, and "actually" by *realmente* or *en realidad:* these are actual facts = *éstos son hechos reales;* I actually did it = *realmente lo hice.* See *efectivo.*

ADVERTENCIA. This is "advice" and not "advertisement". The latter word is *anuncio* in Spanish.

AMERICANO. In Spanish America this word usually means a "Spanish American". A citizen of the United States is called *norteamericano*, or less frequently *estadounidense.* Colloquially "Americans" are known as *yanquis.* Another

11

familiar term is *gringo,* which is heard almost everywhere, but especially in Mexico and Central America where it sometimes carries a depreciative connotation. In South America *gringo* can refer to any kind of foreigner, but usually the fair-haired variety. In Argentina, however, it refers almost exclusively to Italians.

ARGUMENTO. Do not say *tuvimos un argumento* for "we had an argument". This word means a "logical argument", "objection", "proof", etc., and sometimes "summary" or "abstract": *sus argumentos no me convencieron* = his arguments did not convince me. If you mean a "dispute" or "debate", use *disputa:* we had an argument = *tuvimos una disputa.*

ASIGNATURA. This means "course (in school)" and not "signature" *(firma):* explicar *(enseñar* in most of Spanish America) *una asignatura* = to teach a course; *tomar una asignatura* = to take a course. See *curso* and *firma.*

ASISTIR. The usual meaning is "to attend" and not "to assist". Note that *asistir* is always followed by *a:* I attended the class = *asistí a la clase.* "To assist" is best rendered by *ayudar.* See *atender.*

ATENDER. This can only mean "to attend" in the sense of "to take care of", or "attend to". It never has the meaning of "to be present at", which must be translated by *asistir.* Thus: *atiendo a lo que hago* = I am attending to what I am doing; but *asistí a la reunión* = I attended the meeting.

AUDIENCIA. When referring to a group of assembled people, "audience" must be rendered by *auditorio. Audencia* is a "hearing" or an "interview". Thus: *en frente del auditorio* = in front of the audience; *tuve una audiencia con el presidente* = I had an interview with the president.

12

CAPABLE. Here is one word which you should definitely avoid in Spanish. It does not mean "capable", the proper word for which is *capaz*. In fact there is no such word as *capable* in Spanish, but because it appears to be a derivative of the verb *caper*, its use will always cause a good laugh.

CARGA. This is not "charge". If by "charge" you mean "price", say *precio*, if you mean "legal charge" say *acusación*. *Carga* means "burden", "load" or "cargo".

CARGO. This is not the word for "cargo". The correct word is *carga*. *Cargo* means the "act of loading", "care", "assignment", but never "cargo". Thus: *la carga está a mi cargo* = the cargo is in my care.

CHANZA. It is a very amusing error to confuse this word with "chance", although you will find that even some Mexicans, Cubans and Puerto Ricans are guilty of this practice. *Chanza* means "joke", "fun", and *chancear* means "to joke", "to fool". If you mean "chance", say *ocasión*: there will be a chance to speak Spanish = *habrá ocasión de hablar español*. If you want to say "take a chance", use *correr un albur* or *aventurarse*: you will have to take a chance = *Ud. tendrá que correr un albur*.

CIVIL. This is not a noun meaning "civilian", but an adjective. Thus it is impossible to say *un civil* for a "civilian". Use *paisano* instead. Note the correct use of *civil*: the civilians fought for civil rights = *los paisanos pelearon por los derechos civiles*.

COLEGIO. Many people believe that this corresponds to the English "college". The American "college", however, is more advanced than the Spanish *colegio*, and corresponds more closely to the Spanish *universidad*. The *colegio* is a (usually) private school which includes both the elementary and high school grades. You must be careful in these distinctions, otherwise you will not receive your due credit for having graduated from "college".

COLORADO. Strange as it seems, this word cannot mean "colored". The only possible meaning is "red", "reddish", "ruddy". Those who do not know Spanish well say *hombre colorado* for "colored man", but if anything, this would mean "Indian". The idea of "colored" must be expressed by the construction . . . *de color:* colored man = *hombre de color*. Also note the expression *ponerse colorado* = to blush.

CONDUCTOR. This can be a "conductor" only on trains. (The words *revisor* and *inspector* are also used.) A street car or autobus conductor is *cobrador*. In Spain *conductor* is the "motorman" (= *motorista* in Spanish America).
   NOTE: In Mexico *conductor* is used for both the street car and train conductor.

CONEXIÓN. Do not say *tener conexión con* or *conectado con* when you mean "to have connection with" or "connected with". These expressions are used almost exclusively in a mechanical and electrical sense. The correct expressions are *tener relación con* and *estar relacionado con:* he has connections with the bank = *él tiene relaciones con el banco;* I am not connected with the matter = *no tengo relación con el asunto*, or more idiomatically *no tengo nada que ver con el asunto*. Also be careful with the expression "in connection with". There are several ways of saying this in Spanish: *con respecto a, en cuanto a, respecto de* (or *a*), *tocante a*. Remember that "in this connection" would therefore be *con respecto a esto*.

CONFERENCIA. This word can mean "conference", but the more frequent meaning is "lecture", "talk", "speech": *una conferencia de larga distancia* = a long distance call; *el profesor dió una conferencia muy brillante* = the professor gave a very brilliant lecture. See *lectura*.

CONFIDENCIA. This is not "confidence" *(confianza)*, but "something told in confidence". Note the distinction: *me hizo una confidencia* = he told me a secret, but *tengo mucha confianza en él* = I have a lot of confidence in him. *Confianza* can also translate "intimate" in such expressions as: un *amigo de confianza* = an intimate friend; *un tono de confianza* = an intimate tone.

CONSTIPADO. This is not as bad as it appears. *Estar constipado* simply means "to have a cold", and as such is synonymous with *tener un catarro* (or *resfriado)* and *estar acatarrado*. Similarly, *constiparse* means "to catch a cold". which may also be expressed by *resfriarse* or *coger un resfriado*. *Constipación* is therefore not "constipation", but a "cold".

CONTACTO. Avoid this word in reference to persons, for it almost always implies physical contact. When you want to convey the idea of communication, use *comunicación:* I'll contact you tomorrow = *me pondré en comunicación con Ud. mañana;* I got in touch with him by telephone = *me puse en comunicación con él por teléfono.*

CONVENIENTE. This is not "convenient", but "advisable", "suitable", "desirable": *es conveniente hacerlo ahora* = it is advisable to do it now. Render "to be convenient" by *resultar cómodo:* come whenever it is convenient for you = *venga cuando le resulte cómodo;* it is convenient to do

15

it now = *resulta cómodo hacerlo ahora. Cómodo* also
means "comfortable"; see this word in PART II.

COPA. Do not say *una copa de café* for "a cup of coffee".
Copa means a glass with a stem, a goblet, the kind from
which wine is usually drunk. "Cup" is *taza:* a cup of coffee
= *una taza de café.* A "trophy cup", however, is *copa* (because it has a stem): the international cup = *la copa in-
ternacional.* Note that wine is not drunk from a "glass"
(vaso), but from a *copa. Vaso* refers to a "tumbler".

COPIA. This can only mean "copy" when it refers to a
reproduction or an imitation of an original. Thus: *dos
copias de la carta* = two copies of the letter; *él es la copia
de su padre* = he is the image of his father. In all other
cases *ejemplar* must be used: *tengo un ejemplar del libro
(periódico, revista,* etc.) = I have a copy of the book
(newspaper, magazine, etc.). See *ejemplar.*

CORRESPONDIENTE. "Correspondent" is *corresponsal.*
Correspondiente is an adjective meaning "corresponding".
Thus: *mi corresponsal me escribió que tuvo un caso correspondiente* = my correspondent wrote me that he had a
corresponding case. A "co-respondent" in a divorce case is
complice en un caso de divorcio.

CUESTIÓN. A "question" in the sense of an interrogation
is always *pregunta. Cuestión* can be used for "question"
when it means "matter" or "problem": *le hice una pregunta*
= I asked him a question, but: *es una cuestión de dinero*
= it's a question (*i.e.* "matter") of money.

  NOTE: "that is out of the question" = *eso ni pensarlo;*
"the question is to . . ." = *la cuestión está en . . . .*

CURSO. This is not a "course" in school, but the "school
year". A "course" is *asignatura:* I don't want to take this
16

course = *no quiero tomar esta asignatura*. Note the proper use of *curso: un estudiante de primer curso* = a first year student. A "course of study" (comprised of a number of single "courses") is *carrera:* a medical course = *una carrera de medicina*.

NOTE: In Mexico *curso* has come to have the same meaning as *asignatura*.

DESGRACIA. Do not confuse this with "disgrace"; the correct meaning is "misfortune": *¡qué desgracia!* = what a misfortune! A disgrace may be a misfortune, but a misfortune is not always a disgrace. Similarly, *desgraciadamente* is "unfortunately". See *gracia*.

DESHONESTO. Never say *deshonesto* when you mean "dishonest"! These two words convey entirely different ideas. *Deshonesto* is "indecent", "lewd", "immodest". In order to express "dishonest" it is necessary to use the construction *no ser honrado:* this man is dishonest = *este hombre no es honrado*. See *honesto*.

DISGUSTO. This word has a much milder meaning than "disgust". Translate "disgust" by *aversión*. *Disgusto* means "displeasure", "annoyance", "unpleasant experience": *he tenido un disgusto* = I have had an unpleasant experience. Similarly, *disgustar* means "to annoy", "to bother", "to cause displeasure": *él me disgusta* = he bothers me, "he gives me a pain" (not: "he disgusts me" or "I don't like him").

DROGUERÍA. This is not exactly a "drug store". A *droguería* sells such sundries as paints, varnishes, waxes, cleaning materials, perfumes, and toilet articles, as well as drugs and medicine. A "drug store" is either *farmacia* or *botica*.

EDITOR. Despite its appearance, this word can mean only "publisher". "Editor" is *redacto.*. The editor of a particular section of a newspaper is *cronista:* society editor = *cronista de salones (= cronista de sociedad* in Mexico).

NOTE: *casa editorial* = publishing house; *artículo de fondo* = editorial.

EDUCACIÓN. This has a much wider meaning than "education". *Educación* not only includes instruction, but also breeding, social training, and practically all the formative forces in the raising of a child. Thus it corresponds more closely to the English "upbringing". "Education" should be rendered by *instrucción.* Similarly, *educar* means "to raise, bring up", and *instruir* means "to educate": *personas instruídas* = educated people; *personas sin educación* = people without proper upbringing.

EFECTIVO. This means "real" or "actual". "Effective" must be rendered by *eficaz:* the actual facts indicate an effective method = *los hechos efectivos señalan un método eficaz.*

NOTE: In Mexico *efectivo* is used in the sense of "effective" *(= eficaz).* See *actual.*

ELEVADOR. This is not the word for "elevator" or "lift"; say *ascensor.* A freight elevator is *montacargas. Elevador* is an adjective and must be used accordingly: *un mecanismo elevador* = an elevating mechanism.

NOTE: In Mexico *elevador* is used in the sense of "elevator" *(= ascensor).* In Argentina *elevador* means a "grain elevator".

EMBARAZADO. Never use this word to mean "embarrassed"! You will rue the day if you do, for it has one and only one meaning: "pregnant". Use *turbado* or *desconcertado* instead, and above all, never say *estoy embarazado,* for

18

(1) it would be physically impossible, (2) it will give your listeners a good laugh.

ENTRETENER. To express the idea of "entertain", use *divertir:* I entertained her at John's expense = *la divertí a costa de Juan. Entretener* means "to occupy one's attention" or "distract", and contains no suggestion of amusement or pleasure: *durante la pelea la tuve entretenida* = during the fight I kept her attention occupied. Note the expression: *¡no se entretenga!* = do not delay! In some instances *entretener* can mean "to maintain": *entretener una fuerza aérea* = to maintain an air force.

EJEMPLAR. Do not confuse this with *ejemplo* ("example") ; it means "copy". See *copia.*

ÉXITO. This is never "exit"; it means "success". *Tener éxito* = to be successful; *tener mal éxito* = to have little success, to make out badly; *un éxito clamoroso* = a "howling" success. "Exit" is *salida: no tuve éxito en encontrar la salida* = I was unsuccessful in finding the exit.

EXPECTACIÓN. Be careful not to confuse this word with "expectation", which is *esperanza* in Spanish. *Expectación* is "expectancy" or "eagerness": *la expectación del público no colmó nuestras esperanzas* = the eagerness of the public did not come up to our expectations.

FACTORÍA. Do not use this word for "factory" which is *fábrica. Factoría* is a "trading post" or "commercial agency".

NOTE: In Mexico *factoría* is a large factory or "plant".

FACULTAD. You cannot use this word to mean the "faculty of a college or university"; in this sense the correct word is *profesorado:* the faculty is not paid much money = *no se*

19

le paga mucho dinero al profesorado. Facultad in academic circles means a departmental school within a university: *La Facultad de Derecho* = the School of Law. It can also mean a mental or physical faculty: *facultades del alma* = mental faculties.

FAMILIAR. Avoid this word in such expressions as: "I am familiar with him", "a familiar face", etc. Note the following correct renderings:

I am familiar with him = *le conozco*
he is familiar with the matter = *él está enterado del asunto*
a familiar place = *un lugar conocido*

As an adjective, *familiar* means that which pertains to the home and family, and thus "domestic", "homelike", "plain", "simple": *lenguaje familiar* = unceremonious or every-day language. As a noun, *familiar* most frequently means "intimate friend".

FASTIDIOSO. This is not "fastidious" *(melindroso)*, but "annoying" or "boring", "tedious": *él es un tipo muy fastidioso* = he is a very tiresome or bothersome person. Just remember that *fastidioso* comes from the verb *fastidiar* which means "to annoy or bother". Also note *fastidio* = nuisance, bother.

FIRMA. This is not "firm", but "signature" (from *firmar*, "to sign").[1] If you speak of a commercial firm as such, say *casa de comercio* or *casa comercial*; if you wish to mention the name of the firm, follow the formula: *la casa Sánchez y Cía.* (abbreviation of *compañía)* = the firm of Sánchez

---

[1] The meaning of *firma* is well exemplified in the story of a famous Spanish professor, who when signing the register of an American hotel, came to the column entitled "Firm"; *"¡qué tontería!"* he exclaimed, and proceeded to sign his name a second time.

and Company. If by "firm" you mean the name of the firm, use *razón social: nuestra razón social está conocida en toda Sud América* = our firm is known in all South America.

FORMAL. Do not use this when you mean "formal". This word generally means "proper", "sedate", "well-behaved", "serious": *un muchacho formal* = a serious boy. Express the idea of English "formal" by the construction — *de etiqueta:* formal clothes = *traje de etiqueta;* to go formal = *ir de etiqueta.* Thus a "formal dance" would be *baile de etiqueta,* and not *baile formal,* which would be a well-mannered dance, with no misbehavior, excessive drinking or skylarking. It is unnecessary to add that *un baile de etiqueta* is not always *formal!* It is common in conversation to hear your listener say: *¿formal?* = really?, do you mean it?

FÚTIL. If by the English "futile" you mean "ineffective" or "fruitless", use *estéril* in Spanish. *Fútil* means only "trifling", "insignificant": *sus esfuerzos fueron estériles* = his efforts were futile.

GABINETE. This word can mean "cabinet" only when referring to a body of ministers or councillors. If you mean a place for storing various articles, use *armario,* or if a small corner cabinet, *armarito rinconero.* If it is a display cabinet the word is *escaparate (aparador* in Mexico; *vitrina* in parts of South America). *Cabinete* can also mean a "small sitting room", but in Spanish America, at least, this word is considered old fashioned, and *sala* is used instead. Note the expression *estratégico (filósofo* etc.) *de gabinete* = armchair strategist (philosopher etc.). In Spain *gabinete* is the word for "dentist's office"; in most of Spanish America, however, *consultorio dental* (or *de dentista)* is used.

21

GRACIA. Note that this word not only means "grace" but also "joke", "comicalness": *causar* (or *hacer) gracia* = to provoke laughter; *tener gracia* = to be funny, humorous. *¡Qué gracia tiene Juan!* = how humorous John is! When special politeness is desired, *gracia* can also be used for "name (of a person)": *¿cuál es su gracia?* = what is your name?

GRACIOSO. In addition to "graceful" and "gracious", this word also means "amusing", "funny": *¡qué gracioso!* = how funny!

GROSERÍA. No, not grocery! This word means "coarseness", "crude action or speech". Remember that "grocery" is *abacería*, and sometimes *tienda de ultramarinos* (for imported products). In Mexico the word is *tienda de abarrotes* (sometimes *abarrotería)*; in Cuba and Venezuela *bodega;* in Argentina and Uruguay *almacén* (which is a department store elsewhere). In Chile *almacén de abarrotes* is a high grade, luxurious grocery store.[1] Some English speakers make the uncharitable blunder of using *grosero* for "grocer". *Grosero* means "crude", "ill-bred", "vulgar"; translate "grocer" by *abacero* (in Mexico *abarrotero)*.

---

[1] The names for different kinds of stores vary considerably in Spanish America. The most important are: — Mexico: *cajón de ropa* = clothing store (*tienda de ropa), tlapalería* = a kind of hardware store, *pulquería* = place where *pulque* (alcoholic beverage of the Mexican lower classes) is sold; Cuba: *peletería* = shoe store *(zapatería);* Argentina: *mercería* = a kind of dry-goods store, *pulpería* = country general store and bar; Chile: *mercería* = hardware store *(ferretería)*, *despacho* = third rate grocery store for the lower classes. In Argentina, Chile, Cuba and Venezuela *tienda* can mean only a dry-goods store; elsewhere it may refer to a grocery, as in *tienda de comestibles.*

HONESTO. You will not pay the desired compliment if you use *honesto* for "honest", for this means "modest", "decent", "decorous". Express "honest" by *honrado:* an honest man = *un hombre honrado*. Because of English and French influences, even Spaniards sometimes confuse these two words, but the indicated definitions are the only acceptable ones. See *deshonesto*.

INDIANO. If you mean "Indian", say *indio. Indiano* is a resident of Spanish America who originally came from Spain. In the colonial days the word was used by Spaniards to indicate a person who had accumulated wealth in Spanish America and returned to live in Spain.

INFORMACIÓN. Do not confuse this word with "information". *Información* very often means "account" or "report". In newspaper language it is also used to mean "section (of a newspaper)". *Se publicó una amplia información* = a full report was published; *la información deportiva* = the sport section. It is always best to use *informes* for "information": *me pidió informes sobre la información periodística de la conferencia* = he asked me for information on the newspaper account of the conference.

INFORMAL. Not "informal", but the opposite of *formal,* that is, "unconventional", "not done according to the rules and regulations". Therefore *un baile informal* would be a brawling and immoderate affair. For "informal" use such expressions as *sin ceremonia:* he received me informally = *me recibió sin ceremonia*. See *formal*.

INTRODUCIR. By all means avoid this word when you mean "to introduce a person". *Introducir* means "to introduce" only in a physical sense, that is, "to insert": *él introdujo el dedo en el agujero* = he put his finger in the

23

hole. When you mean "introduce a person" always use *presentar:* I introduced him to my father = *le presenté a mi padre.*

LABOR. This word has a much wider meaning than the English "labor". It can mean any kind of work, either mental or manual: *la labor de este autor es señalada* = the work of this author is notable. "Labor" as an economic concept is rendered by *trabajo:* capital and labor = *capitalismo y trabajo.*

LECTURA. This word has only one meaning: "reading". Translate "lecture" by *conferencia:* the professor gave a lecture on certain selected readings = *el profesor dió una conferencia sobre ciertas lecturas escogidas.* See *conferencia.*

LIBRERÍA. This is not "library" but "book store". Remember that "library" is always *biblioteca.*

LUJURIA. At all cost, do not mistake this word for "luxury"; the meaning is *very* different: "lewdness", "lust", "physical excess". Translate "luxury" by *lujo.* The same distinction applies to *lujurioso* (lusty, lewd, voluptuous) and *lujoso* (luxurious, lavish). To be *lujurioso* and *lujoso* are two very different things!

MANERAS. This word cannot be used when speaking of "social manners". *Manera* is a "way of doing something": *su manera de hablar* = his way of speaking. "Social manners" must be rendered by *modales:* his manners are bad = *sus modales son malos* (not *maneras*). Note the expressions with *manera: de manera que* (followed by the subjunctive) = "so", or "so that". So you're going to Cuba! = *¡de manera que vas a Cuba!* I speak so that he can

24

understand = *hablo de manera que me entienda.* He did it in his own way = *lo hizo a su manera.*[1]

MATRIMONIO. The most usual meaning is "married couple": *un matrimonio vive en esta casa* = a married couple lives in this house. For "matrimony" it is best to use *casamiento.*

MOTIVO. This word means "ground", "cause", "reason", and not "motive": grounds for divorce = *motivos de divorcio.* Express "motive" by *móvil:* motives for crime = *móviles de crimen.*

NATIVO. You cannot use this word to mean "native"; use *natural* instead: *es natural de la Argentina* = he is a native of Argentina (never: *es nativo de la Argentina*). *Nativo* is an adjective and must be used in such constructions as: *mi lengua nativa* = my native language. If you wish to speak of native tribes, animals etc., use *aborigen* or *indígena:* the (original) natives of Mexico = *los indígenas de Méjico.*[2]

NATURAL. Remember that in addition to "natural", this word also means "native". See *nativo.*

NOTICIA. Do not confuse this with "notice". *Noticia* is a "piece of news", and in the plural *(noticias)* it means "news": *voy a comunicarle una noticia interesante* = I am

---

[1] *Manera* (and *modo*) may take the prepositions *de, a* or *en; a* is used when indicating the manner of an individual person: *a su manera* = in his own way. *De* is used in most other cases: *de esta manera* = in this way; *de ninguna manera* = by no means; *de todas maneras* = in any case.

[2] In Mexico the official spelling is *México* and *mexicano.* Elsewhere, however, *Méjico* and *mejicano* are used. The pronunciation in either case is always that of *j.*

25

going to let you in on an interesting piece of news. Translate "notice" by *aviso*: did you see the notice on the bulletin board? = *¿vió Ud. el aviso en el tablón* (in Mexico *tablero*)? If you mean "notification", use *notificación*. Similarly, *noticiar* means "to give notice"; translate "to notice" by *notar*, *fijarse en* or *reparar en*: did you notice his suit? *¿reparó Ud. en su traje?*

OCASIÓN. This is not "occasion" in the sense of "event", but is the usual word for "opportunity": *aprovechar una ocasión* = to take advantage of an opportunity. By extension *ocasión* has also come to mean "bargain". Note the expression: – *de ocasión* = second hand: *un libro de ocasión* = a second hand book. If you mean "event", use *acontecimiento* or *suceso*. See *suceso*.

OCURRENCIA. This word is seldom used nowadays to mean "occurrence". The usual meaning is either "witty saying" or "idea": *su ocurrencia me hizo reír* = his witticism made me laugh; *¡qué ocurrencia suya!* = what a bright idea of yours!; *¡qué ocurrencia tan rara!* = what a strange idea! It is helpful to remember that *ocurrencia* is something which "occurs" *(ocurrir)* to mind. A person who has *ocurrencias* is said to be *ocurrente*: what a clever (in a witty sense) fellow! = *¡qué tipo tan ocurrente!* If you want to say "occurrence", use *caso, incidente* or *acaecimiento*: that is a frequent occurrence = *eso es un caso frecuente;* such occurrences are to be expected = *tales incidentes son de esperar.*

OFICIAL. This cannot mean "official" when used as a noun. An "official" is *funcionario* or *dignatario*. As a noun *oficial* means "officer"; only as an adjective can it mean "official". Note the correct use: *el oficial ejecutó muchos actos oficiales* = the officer performed many official acts.

OFICIO. Do not confuse this with the English word "office", which is *oficina* or *despacho* in Spanish. (For special kinds of "office", see *office* in Part II.) *Oficio* is "job" or "occupation", and is usually manual, that is a "craft" or "trade": *él tiene un oficio muy duro* = he has a very hard job.

ORDINARIO. In Spanish this word has two meanings: (1) "ordinary", "everyday", (2) "coarse", "unrefined". To avoid any misunderstandings, it is advisable to use *corriente* when you wish to express the first meaning: *el hombre corriente* = the ordinary (common) man.

PARIENTE. You will not be understood if you speak of your parents as *parientes*, for this word means "family relatives." Translate "parents" by *padres*. The Spanish usage is well demonstrated in the story of the Spanish American who, on inquiring about a friend's parents, asked: "–and how are your fathers?" Note that a male relative is *el pariente* and that a female relative is *la parienta*. See *relativo* and *relación*.

PARTICULAR. This is not "particular" but "private": *una casa particular* = a private house; *lecciones particulares* = private lessons. Note that *un particular* is a "private person". If by "particular" you mean the adjective, say *cierto*: a particular day = *cierto día*. If you mean the noun, use *detalles* (details): *le mando los detalles* = I am sending you the particulars. See *privado*.

PLANTA. Even some Spanish speaking people make the mistake (through the influence of English) of using this word for "plant" in the sense of a "factory". The correct word is *fábrica; central* is usually used for electric power

27

plants: *un central eléctrico* = an electric power plant.[1] In correct Spanish *planta* refers only to botanical plants.

POPULACIÓN. Observe that this is not "population", but "the act of populating": *la populación de esta región ofreció muchas dificultades* = the populating of this region presented many difficulties. The English "population" should be rendered by *pueblo*.

POSICIÓN. It is best to avoid this word in such expressions as: "to be in a position (to do something)", "his position in the matter is unknown", etc. *Posición* means only "physical position", and must be used accordingly: *estaba sentado en posición incómoda* = he was seated in an uncomfortable position. In other cases use *condición* or *situación*: I am not in a position to do it = *no estoy en condición de hacerlo*.

PRÁCTICAMENTE. You cannot use this word in such sentences as: "he knows practically nothing", "it was practically a failure" etc., where "practically" means "almost", "really". *Prácticamente* means "through experience": *hemos sabido prácticamente* = we have learned through experience. Express the English "practically" in such cases by *casi, realmente* or *efectivamente:* he was practically "broke" = *estaba casi arrancado*.

PRETENDER. This is not "pretend"; it means "to seek", "to try to": *él pretendió robarme* = he sought to rob me. Translate "pretend" by *fingir:* he pretended to know = *fingió saber*.

PRIVADO. This word has a much narrower meaning than English "private". The most common translation is "per-

---

[1] In Cuba *central* is the native word for "sugar mill".

sonal": *limpieza privada* = personal cleanliness; *corres-pondencia privada* = personal mail. Remember that "private" is *particular* in Spanish. See *particular*.

PROCURAR. It is true that this word can mean "to procure", but in addition it also very çommonly means "to try", "to endeavor": *procuró encontrar el dinero* = he tried to find the money.

PROPAGANDA. This word not only means "propaganda", but it is also the common word for "advertising": *la casa gastó un dineral en propaganda* = the firm spent a fortune on advertising. Note that "advertisement" is *aviso* or *anuncio,* and that "to advertise" is *anunciar. Insertar un anuncio en el periódico* = to put an advertisement in the newspaper. See *advertencia.*

PUNTUAL. This word means more than merely "punctual". The closest translation would be "accurate", "precise": *datos puntuales* = accurate facts. The same applies to *puntualmente* and *puntualidad:* he did everything very faithfully = *lo hizo todo muy puntualmente;* he described the situation with great accuracy = *describió la situación con gran puntualidad.*

REALIZAR. Do not use this word in the usual sense of "realize". *Realizar* means "to carry out" or "to perform": *realizó su proyecto* = he carried out his plan; *realizaré mi promesa* = I shall keep my promise. In a commercial sense it means "to sell at a profit" *(i.e.* "to realize on") : *la casa realizó todas sus mercancías* = the firm converted all its merchandise into cash. Also note the commercial expression: *realizar ganancias* = to gain profits. (Note: In Mexico the more usual expression is *obtener ganancias.)* If by "realize" you mean "to understand", "to take into consideration", use such expressions as *darse cuenta de* and *hacerse cargo de:* he did not realize his error = *no se dió cuenta* (or: *no se hizo cargo*) *de su error*.

REGULAR. You will avoid many misunderstandings if you remember that this word not only means "regular", but also "average", "moderate", "ordinary": *una casa de tamaño regular* = an average sized house. In answers to questions *regular* frequently corresponds to the English "so, so", "fair-to-middling".

RELACIÓN. This word cannot be used to mean "relation" in the sense of "kinsfolk". The correct word is *pariente:* my relations speak Spanish = *mis parientes hablan español*. Note how to express "related to (by marriage or birth)": *estar emparentado con*; thus *estoy emparentado con ella* = I am related to her. *Relaciones* means "relations" in the sense of mutual dealings and interests: *mis relaciones con mis parientes son muy amistosas* = my dealings ("relations") with my relations are very friendly. See *pariente* and *relativo*.

RELATIVO. This word does not mean "family relations", which must be *parientes* in Spanish. *Relativo* is "relative" only as an adjective meaning "that which is in relation to": *nuestras situaciones relativas* = our relative positions; *el valor relativo* = the relative value; *pronombre relativo* = relative pronoun. See *relación* and *pariente*.

REMARCAR. Not "to remark", but "to mark again". Express "to remark" by *observar, advertir* or *notar*.

RESORTE. Be careful not to use this word when referring to a "vacation resort"; *lugar de veraneo* is the correct word. *Resorte* means "resources", "means" and in mechanical terminology, "spring". Note how to express "as a last resort': *en último caso.*

SALARIO. This is not "salary". *Salario* is the money paid only to servants and laborers, and thus corresponds to the English "wages". "Salary" is *sueldo.*

SENSIBLE. This is never "sensible". The two most frequent meanings are: (1) "sensitive", (2) "perceptible" or "appreciable": *ella es muy sensible* = she is very sensitive; *alteraciones sensibles* = perceptible changes. Translate "sensible" by *sensato, razonable* or the expression — *de buen sentido:* he is a sensible person = *él es una persona de buen sentido* (or: *sensata, razonable*). Note the idiom: *¡póngase en razón!* = be sensible!

SENTENCIA. This means "sentence" only in the legal sense of a "court sentence". When referring to a group of words, however, use *frase* or in grammatical context, *oración.*

SERIO. In addition to the English "serious", this word also very commonly means "reliable": *un médico serio* = a reliable doctor. It is very often used in the expression *cosa seria* to mean "worth while": *este libro es cosa seria* = this book is worth while. In the sense of "serious", *grave* is perhaps more usual than *serio:* a very serious illness = *una enfermedad muy grave.* When you mean "serious minded", use *formal:* a serious (minded) boy = *un muchacho formal.* See *formal.*

SIMPÁTICO. This is one of the most important words in the Spanish language, and one whose meaning you should learn at the very start. It is by no means "sympathetic". The exact meaning is somewhat elusive and difficult to define, but it corresponds roughly to "pleasant", "nice", or the slang use of "swell" when applied to persons. To be called *simpático* by a Spaniard or a Spanish American is a great compliment, for it means you have won a place in their affections.

SUCESO. Remember that this word has nothing to do with "success", which is *éxito* in Spanish. *Suceso* means "happening" or "minor event". Similarly, *suceder* means "to happen", "to occur": *¿qué sucedió?* = what happened? See *ocurrencia,* and *event* in Part II.

SUJETO. It is advisable to avoid this word when you mean "subject", unless you are speaking of the "subject of a sentence". *Sujeto* usually means "fellow", "person": *no conozco a este sujeto* = I don't know this person.

NOTE: Avoid this use of *sujeto* in the Argentine, for there it is depreciative and insulting.

Observe the following translations of "subject":

he is a subject of Mexico = *es súbdito de Méjico*

on what subject is he speaking? = *¿sobre qué tema habla?*

what subjects are you studying? = *¿qué materias estudia Ud.?*

TIPO. In addition to "type", "pattern", "model" etc., this word is very extensively used in colloquial speech to mean "fellow" or "guy": *¿quién es este tipo?* = who is this guy?

NOTE: There are many local words for "guy", of which the most notable are: *gallo* or *pájaro* (Chile, Peru, Ecuador etc.), *pisco* (Colombia); the Cubans and Puerto Ricans are especially fond of *chico,* and the Spaniards like *tío* ("uncle").

II. THESE DISCRIMINATING LATINS!

In ENGLISH we frequently use the same word to cover several variants of an idea. For example, think of the verb "to get" and all the meanings which it has. Spanish, on the other hand, is very sensitive to distinctions in meaning and distinguishes such variants by using a different word for each of them. It is important to realize that for the native speaker these distinctions usually represent completely separate ideas. You must not think that we are "splitting hairs"; to the Spanish mind the difference between the Spanish equivalents for "get" in the expressions "to get sick" and "to get a letter" is as great as that between *hablar* and *escribir*.

Each of the following English words has several Spanish renditions, depending upon the particular idea which you wish to convey. It is a good plan to train yourself to appreciate these distinctions from the very beginning, for this ability will make all the difference in the world between frowns of misunderstanding and nods of agreement on the faces of your Spanish listeners.

AGREE

estar (quedar) de acuerdo con = "to be in agreement with". This merely indicates that agreement exists: *estoy de acuerdo con Ud.* = I agree with you.

ponerse de acuerdo = "to come to an agreement". This indicates that there has previously been a lack of agreement: *nos ponemos de acuerdo* = we are coming to an agreement.

33

quedar en = "to agree on (to)". This implies merely that an agreement is made with no previous divergence of opinion: *quedamos en vernos al día siguiente* = we agreed to meet the following day.

convenir en = "to come to an agreement on (to)". This implies that there has previously been a lack of agreement: *convinimos en el precio* = we agreed on the price (after an argument perhaps).

BEAT

golpear = "to give blows to". This implies the giving of repeated blows: *golpeó al preso con un azote* = he beat the prisoner with a whip.

batir = "to batter or pound". This conveys the idea of smashing or pounding: *batió la pared con las manos* = he beat the wall with his hands.

> NOTE: *batir el record (de boletería)* = to beat the (box-office) record.

pegar = "to flog, spank". This implies that punishment is involved: *se le pegó al muchacho* = the boy was given a thrashing. Note that *pegar* also means "to stick", "to fasten". *Pegar fuego a* = to set fire to.

BECOME

The English verb "to become" is also expressed by such verbs as "to grow" (to grow old), "to get" (to get sick), "to get to be" (to get to be president) and "to turn" (to turn cold). In Spanish there are at least five separate translations of the English verb.

hacerse = "to become + noun or adjective". In regard to persons this verb indicates that the subject has acted voluntarily and with intention (remember that *hacerse* really means "to make one's self") : *se hizo médico* = he became a doctor; *se ha hecho rico* = he has become rich. *Hacerse* is also used to indicate impersonal "becoming": *se hace tarde* = it's getting late (contrast to *es tarde* = it is late) ; *el río se hizo más ancho* = the river became wider.

ponerse = 'to become + adjective". This implies involuntary or unintentional action. It is usually used with adjectives describing emotional and physical conditions: *se puso rojo* = he turned red (i.e. "blushed") ; *Ud. se pondrá mojado* = you will get wet; *se ha puesto gordo* = he has become fat.

> NOTE: The cumulative idea of "getting to be" and "becoming" may be expressed by using *irse* with *hacer* and *poner* in accordance with the above distinctions in meaning: he is getting fat = *se va poniendo gordo;* the heat is getting intolerable = *el calor se va haciendo insoportable;* he is getting rich = *se va haciendo rico.*

llegar (or *venir) a ser* = "to become + noun". Although this construction conveys the same sense of personal effort and volition as does *hacerse*, it may also imply great accomplishment: *llegó a ser gerente de la casa* = he got to be manager of the firm.

volverse = "to turn + noun or adjective". This verb stresses the change from one condition to another: *se volvió loco* = he went mad; *se volvió médico* = he turned doctor; *la leche se ha vuelto* = the milk has "turned" (sour).

ser de = "to become of". This construction is used in such expressions as: what has become of John? = *¿qué ha sido de Juan?;* what will become of me? = *¿qué será de mí?*

35

NOTE: In Spanish there are many verbs which contain the idea of becoming. Some of these are characterized by the ending *–ecer*.

envejecer = to grow old
enriquecerse = to get rich
enrojecerse = to turn red
empobrecerse = to become poor
enfadarse = to get angry
emborracharse = to get drunk

calentarse = to get hot
casarse = to get married
enfermar = to get sick
mejorarse = to get better
disponerse = to get ready
perderse = to get lost

BEGIN

The most common verbs are *empezar* and *ponerse a*. *Comenzar* is the more literary word. The following deserve special attention:

echarse a: this supposes the existence of an emotional state: *se echó a llorar* = he began to cry (i.e. "he broke out crying").

echar a: this is used with verbs of motion and conveys the idea of a sudden start: *echó a correr* = he began to run *(i.e.* "he broke into a run").

BOAT

bote = small boat propelled by oars and holding two or three persons.

barca = somewhat larger than *bote;* used for coastal sailing and may carry sails.

barco }
buque } = ship

vapor = steamship

BURN

quemar = "to cause to burn" (transitive verb): *el fósforo quema la mesa* = the match is burning the table.

arder = "to be in a state of burning" (intransitive verb): *el fósforo arde* = the match is burning.

CHANGE

When speaking of money, you must distinguish between two kinds of "change", otherwise you will have misunderstandings with the cashier.

vuelta (*vuelto* in Spanish America) This is the money which you get back after your payment has been taken out: *déme la vuelta* = give me my change.

suelto = money in small denominations: *no tengo suelto* = I have no change.

COMFORTABLE

Be careful to distinguish between the following two constructions:

estar cómodo is used in reference to persons. *Estar bien* or *estar a gusto* may also be used. I am comfortable = *estoy cómodo* (or *bien* or *a gusto*).

ser cómodo is used in reference to furniture and other inanimate objects: *esta butaca es muy cómoda* = this chair is very comfortable.

COST

costa = "expense", particularly in the legal sense: *tuve que pagar las costas del juicio* = I had to pay the expenses of the trial; *a su costa* = at his expense; *a toda costa* = at any cost.

coste (or *costo*) = "price": *el coste del libro ha ascendido* = the price of the book has gone up.

CORNER

esquina = "outside corner": *la esquina de la calle* = the corner of the street.

rincón = "inside corner": *el rincón del cuarto* = the corner of the room.

DAMAGE

daño = "physical damage or injury": *me hace daño* = it hurts me; *el auto sufrió daños* = the car suffered damages.

desperfectos = "slight physical damages".

perjuicio = "moral or abstract damage". The verb is *perjudicar:* to damage one's reputation = *perjudicar la reputación de uno;* to hurt one's name = *perjudicar el nombre de uno.*

DATE

In colloquial English we often use the word "date" to mean an "engagement"; be careful not to do this in Spanish:

fecha = "date of time".

cita or *compromiso* = "engagement".

> NOTE: In those Spanish American countries near the United States, you will sometimes hear *un date* (pronounced as in English), because it is more colorful and sophisticated.

DRIVE

In Spanish there is no single equivalent for "to drive". See *walk* and *ride.*

manejar or *conducir* = "to act as a driver", "to drive (a vehicle)": *¿sabe Ud. manejar auto?* = can you drive a car? In Spanish America *manejar* is more frequent than *conducir.*

pasearse en auto[1] = "to take a drive (for diversion)": *¿quisiera Ud. pasearse en auto?* = would you like to take a drive?

---

[1] The word for "car", "automobile", varies somewhat in different parts of Spanish America. Cuba and Puerto Rico use *máquina* and *carro;* Mexico prefers *coche* and *carro.* In most other places, *coche* and *auto* are used.

38

ir en auto = "to drive (in opposition to walking or riding horse)": *¿quisiera Ud. ir en auto o a pie?* = do you want to drive or walk?

ir a pasearse (paseo) en auto = "to go for a drive": *¡vamos a pasearnos en auto!* = let's go for a drive!

EVENT

acontecimiento = "event", a major and memorable experience: *para mí era un acontecimiento* = for me it was an event.

suceso = "happening", a minor experience or "incident". The word *incidente* has about the same meaning: *estos sucesos* (or *incidentes) pasan muy frecuentemente* = these incidents happen very frequently.

EXCUSE ME

The use of the various Spanish expressions for "excuse me" is one of the most frequent pitfalls of Americans. Each expression in Spanish has a certain situation in which it must be used. Disregard for such conditions will make your intended courtesies appear ridiculous.

dispénseme or *perdone:* you should use these expressions to excuse yourself when you have already committed some discourteous act, or when you wish to broach an inquiry or intrude. *Perdone* is somewhat more polite. If, for instance, you should accidently step on some one's foot, you would say "*¡oh, perdóneme Ud., por favor!*"

con (su) permiso: you should use this expression when begging pardon for something which you are about to do. If, for example, you must leave your guests for a moment, you should say "*con (su) permiso*". This courtesy is resorted to whenever you take any liberty which requires a perfunctory approval. It would be ludicrous to use this after a discourteous act has been committed.

GET

Great care should be taken with the translation of the English "get". It has no equivalent in Spanish and must be rendered in various ways. In general there are five central meanings:

(1) *obtain, procure (get + noun)*

obtener: he gets good marks = *obtiene buenas notas*
conseguir: he got what he wanted = *consiguió lo que quería*
coger: where can I get the train? = *¿dónde puedo coger el tren?*

> NOTE: Avoid the verb *coger* in Argentina and Chile, since it has acquired another meaning. See introductory "A Word to the Wise".

tomar: I am going to get a taxi = *voy a tomar un taxi*
encontrar: I couldn't get it = *no podía encontrarlo*
traer: get me the book = *tráigame el libro*
buscar: go get me a newspaper = *vaya a buscarme un periódico*
comprar: I couldn't get a dress = *no podía comprar un vestido.*

(2) *become (get + adjective)*

When followed by an adjective, "to get" is equivalent to "become". For the various renditions of this idea, see *become*.

(3) *motion (get + preposition or adverb)*

llegar a = to get to: *llegaré a casa a las ocho* = I'll get home at eight

ir a = to get to: *¿por dónde se va a la ciudad?* = how do you get to the city?

entrar = to get in: *¿por dónde se entra?* = how do you get in?

salir = to get out: *¿por dónde se sale de aquí?* = how do you get out of here?

sacar = to get (a thing) out: *no puedo sacarlo* = I can't get it out

subir a = to get up on (in) to: *subí al tranvía* = I got onto the streetcar

bajar de = to get down from: *bajó del tren* = he got down off the train

escaparse = to get away: *se escapó* = he got away

levantarse = to get up: *me levanto a las seis* = I get up at six o'clock

regresar = to get back (return): *regresaré pronto* = I'll get back soon

recobrar = to get back (receive): *no lo recobré* = I didn't get it back

reunirse = to get together: *ayer nos reunimos* = we got together yesterday.

(4) condition (get + adverb)

ir pasando = to get along (health, affairs, etc.)

ir tirando = to get by (health, affairs, etc.)

adelantarse = to get ahead

defenderse = to get along well (with, in something)

acabar = to get done, finished

comunicarse con = to get in touch with

deshacerse (librarse) de = to get rid of

descomponerse = to get out of order.

(5) to succeed in getting (get + infinitive)

This type of construction is best rendered by *lograr* + *infinitive:* he got to go = *logró ir;* I'll get to see him =

41

lograré verle; he didn't get in *(i.e.* "he didn't succeed in getting in") = *no logró entrar.*

NOTE: Do not forget that "have got to" must be rendered by *tener que:* I have got to go = *tengo que ir.*

GO

andar applies to the motion of animals and inanimate objects. With regard to persons it indicates indefinite and aimless motion: *él anduvo de prisa por la calle* = he went rapidly through the street; *el reloj no anda bien* = the watch doesn't go well; *el perro anda a gatas* = the dog goes on all fours.

ir implies a specific direction and purpose. This is the most frequent rendition: *voy a Cuba* = I'm going to Cuba; *¿a dónde va Ud.?* = where are you going?

NOTE: "I am coming" in answer to a call is *ya voy* or *allá voy.*

Certain verbs contain the idea of "go"; note especially the following:

bajar = go down	*atravesar* = to go over
subir = to go up	*acostarse* = to go to bed
entrar = to go into	*volver* = to go back
salir = to go out	*dormirse* = to go to sleep
acompañar = to go with	*apagarse* = to go out
pasar = to go past	(lights, fires)

CUEST

Your guest will misinterpret his position unless you are careful to use the proper word:

huésped = a "house-guest" or "lodger".

NOTE: *casa de huéspedes* = boarding house.

42

convidado (or *invitado*) This is a guest in the sense of an invited person, and is therefore by far the most frequent rendition. Thus when offering to pay for your friend's dinner, "you are my guest" should be translated *Ud. es mi convidado*, or more idiomatically, *yo le convido*.

HERE

See *there*.

HIT

See *beat* and *strike*.

HOW

The rendering of "how" is a great stumbling block for the student. The following treatment should help clarify this difficulty.

(1) *In Exclamations*

(a) Before an adjective or adverb:
   qué or *cuán:* how small it is! = *¡qué (cuán) pequeño es!*; how well he plays! = *¡qué (cuán) bien toca!*; how late it is! = *¡qué tarde es!*; see how sad he is! = *¡mire qué triste viene!* NOTE: *Cuán* is a literary form.

(b) Before verbs:
   cómo: how he runs! = *¡cómo corre!* If you mean "how much" use *cuánto:* how your sister has changed! = *¡cuánto ha cambiado su hermana!*; how much he knows! = *¡cuánto sabe!*

(2) *In Statements*

(a) Before an adjective or adverb:
   cuán or *lo + adjective + que:* I know how long it is = *sé cuán largo (lo largo que) es*; you have no idea of

43

how difficult the lesson is = *Ud. no tiene idea de lo difícil que es la lección.*[1]

(b) Before verbs:

cómo: I don't know how he does it = *no sé cómo lo hace.*

(3) *In Questions*

(a) Before an adjective or adverb:

There is no single equivalent for "how" in such cases, and it must be rendered by various expressions:

how often? = *¿cada cuánto?* or *¿cuántas veces?*	how soon? = *¿cuándo?*
	how late? = *¿a qué hora?*
how fast? = *¿con qué velocidad?*	how long? (time) = *¿cuánto tiempo?*
how far? = *¿a qué distancia?*	how so? = *¿cómo así?*

Before adjectives of dimension, several formulas are available:

cómo es de + *adjective: ¿cómo es de largo el camino?*

qué + *adjective* + *tiene: ¿qué largo tiene el camino?* ⎬ how long is the road?

cuán + *adjective* + *es: ¿cuán largo es el camino?*

The first formula is more common in Spain, while Spanish America usually prefers the second.

NOTE: In Mexico the formula is *qué tan* + *adjective or adverb:* how long is the road? = *¿qué tan largo es el camino?*

---

[1] Note that although in this construction *lo* is invariable (neuter), the following adjective agrees with its noun: "I know how rich he is" = *sé lo rico que es él;* but "I know how rich she is" = *sé lo rica que es ella.*

In most other cases the most convenient rendition is to use a definite question: *¿es muy emociante?* = how exciting is it?; *¿es el libro muy interesante?* = how interesting is the book?

(b) Before a verb:

In many cases Spanish makes an important distinction, depending upon the kind of information desired.

cómo: asks by what *procedure* a thing is done. The answer involves a description of *how to do* the act:

> *¿Cómo conduce Ud. auto?* = How do you drive a car? *(i.e.* what things do you do to drive a car?)

> *¿Cómo lo hace?* = How does he do it? *(i.e.* what method does he use?)

qué tal: asks *in what manner* a thing is done. The answer involves some qualifying or descriptive adverb:

> *¿Qué tal conduce Ud. auto?* = How do you drive a car? *(i.e.* well, badly, carefully, recklessly, etc.)

> *¿Qué tal lo hace?* = How does he do it? *(i.e.* does he do it well, competently, thoroughly, with ease, badly, etc.)

In some cases (frequently with *ser* and *estar)* no distinction can be made and both *qué tal* and *cómo* may be used interchangeably: *¿cómo (qué tal) está Ud.?* = how are you? In such instances *qué tal* is considered more colloquial.

> NOTE: In asking for directions, you should translate "how" by *por dónde* when you want to know what route to follow. Observe the different meanings with *cómo* and *qué tal:*

> *¿Por dónde va el auto?* = By what route does the car go?

> *¿Cómo va el auto?* = How does the car go (by what mechanism)?

¿Qué tal va el auto? = How does the car go (smoothly, fast, etc.) ?

HOW DO YOU LIKE?

In English this expression can mean one of three things, each of which is distinguished in Spanish and rendered differently:

¿Qué (tal) le parece?
¿Qué tal le gusta?

These ask for an opinion, and are the most frequent rendering of the English "how do you like": *¿Qué (tal) le parece la sopa?* = *¿Qué tal le gusta la sopa?* = How do you like (What do you think of) the soup? *(i.e.,* do you think it is tasty, too hot, well prepared, etc.) Still another expression would be: *¿Cómo encuentra Ud. la sopa?*

¿Cómo le gusta? This asks in what manner a thing is liked best: *¿Cómo le gusta la sopa?* = how (in what way) do you like the soup? *(i.e.,* with lots of salt, hot, with less seasoning, etc.) You cannot use this expression to mean "what do you think of . . ."

¿Le gusta? This asks whether a thing is liked or not. The answer must entail a "yes" or "no" reply. *¿Le gusta la sopa?* = Do you like the soup?

INTEREST(ED)

interesar = "to be interested in". This verb is used with the third person construction: *su trabajo me interesa* = I am interested in his work.

estar interesado en = "to have an interest (financial) in": *estoy interesado en su negocio* = I have an interest (investment) in his business.

interesarse en can mean either of the above definitions.

46

interesarse por = "to take an active interest in". This is stronger than *interesar:* I take a great interest in the arts = *me intereso por las artes.*

LEARN

aprender = to learn through study

averiguar = "to learn" in the sense of "find out": *averigüé donde está* = I learned where he is.

saber = in the preterite (past) and perfect tenses this means "learned" in the sense of "find out". This usage is very common: *¿dónde ha sabido Ud. eso?* = where did you learn (find out) that?; *supe eso en la Habana* = I learned (found out) that in Havana.

NOTE: The past of "know" must be expressed by the imperfect: *no lo sabía* = I didn't know it.

LEAVE

salir = "to leave" in the sense of "depart": *¿cuándo sale el tren?* = when does the train leave?

dejar = "to leave" in the sense of "to leave a thing or person" (*i.e.* transitive verb): *me dejó en la esquina* = he left me on the corner; *¡déjame en paz!* = leave me alone! Note that *dejar por* + *infinitive* translates the English "to leave un- + past participle": *lo dejó por escribir* = he left it unwritten; *lo dejó por hacer* = he left it undone.

quedar = "to be left": *quedé a solas* = I was left alone; *él quedó huérfano* = he was left an orphan. When you mean "to be left over", use either *quedar* or *restar:* I have two pesos left (over) = *me quedan* (or *restan) dos pesos;* there is one piece left = *queda un pedazo.* See *remain.*

47

LOAN

empréstito = large loan, usually between companies and countries.

préstamo = smaller loan, usually between individuals.

NOTE: The popular expression "to hit some one for a loan" is *darle a uno un sablazo* in Spanish: *traté de darle un sablazo a Juan* = I tried to "hit John for a loan". In Argentina *pechar* is used, while in Cuba it is *darle a uno una brava*.

LOOK

mirar = "to look at" (note that "at" is contained in the verb and is not translated): *yo estaba mirando el cuadro* = I was looking at the picture; *¡mire!* = look!

NOTE: In some parts of Spanish America *¡fíjese!* is preferred to *¡mire!* Observe the idioms: *dar una mirada* (or *un vistazo) a* = *echar una ojeada a* = to take a look (glance) at.

parecer = "to look" in the sense of "appear": *parece que va a llover* = it looks as if it will rain; *parece bueno* = it looks good.

parecerse a = "to look like": *él se parece a su padre* = he looks like his father.

tener cara de = "to look like"; used when speaking of the physical attributes of persons: *Ud. tiene cara de no haber dormido* = you look like you have not slept; *él tiene cara de buena persona* = he looks like a nice person.

asomarse a = 'to look out of": *me asomé a la ventana* = I looked out of the window.

tener cuidado con = "to look out for": *¡tenga cuidado con los rateros!* = look out for pickpockets!

buscar = "to look for": *busco el libro* = I am looking for the book.

examinar = "to look over, through": *examinó el pasaporte* = he looked over the passport.

hojear = "to look through (a book, magazine etc.)". This word is used with anything that has pages *(hojas)*: *él estaba hojeando el libro* = he was looking ("thumbing") through the book.

MAIL BOX

buzón = the mail box in which letters are placed when they are mailed.

apartado = the mail box in which you receive letters; it may be either a post office box or the one located at your home.

NOTE: In Argentina and Chile *apartado* means "paragraph", and *casilla (de correo)* is used instead.

MATCH

cerilla Strictly speaking this is a wax match. In Spain, however, it is used almost exclusively for all kinds of matches; the word *fósforo* is not very frequent.

NOTE: In Mexico the form is *cerillo*.

fósforo Strictly speaking this is a wooden or cardboard match. In most of Spanish America, however, it is used for all kinds of matches, including *cerillas*.

MEET

encontrar
tropezar con } = {
dar con

"to meet by chance", that is, "to run across": *tropecé (di) con él en la calle* = *le encontré en la calle* = I ran across him in the street. Note that *encontrar* may also mean "to find".

49

verse con = "to meet by arrangement": *¿cuándo se verá Ud. con ella?* = when are you going to meet her?

conocer = "to meet" in the sense of make the acquaintance: *tanto gusto en conocerle* = it's a pleasure to meet you. The preterite must be used to convey the past of this meaning: *le conocí en la Habana* = I met (got to know) him in Havana. Note the meaning of the imperfect tense: *le conocía en la Habana* = I knew him in Havana.

reunirse = "to meet" in the sense that a group convenes: *los estudiantes siempre se reúnen aquí* = the students always meet here.

MISS

perder This is used when you mean "not to get something which you want or have been waiting for". It is used in such expressions as "to miss a train, show, road" etc.: *perdí la primera función* = I missed the first show.

echar de menos Use this when you mean "to have a longing for": *él echa de menos a su esposa* = he misses his wife.

> NOTE: In Mexico, Central America and in parts of Andean South America, *extrañarle a alguien* is also used: *él extraña a su esposa.*

When you mean that you did not notice something or some one, use *no ver* or *perder de ver:* I missed (seeing) the accident = *no vi el accidente.*

MOVE

mover = "to cause to move" (transitive verb). This indicates a change of position without specifying a definite direction or place: *mueva su brazo* = move your arm.

moverse = "to move" (intransitive verb). This means that the subject itself is moving; *¡no se mueva!* = don't move!; *se mueve fácilmente* = it moves easily.

50

desplazar = "to move" (from one position to another). This implies a specific direction of movement: *se desplazó de un lado a otro* = he moved from one side to the other.

mudarse = "to move" in the sense of "change residence": *vamos a mudarnos (de casa) mañana* = we are going to move tomorrow.

correr = "to move (something) over": *corra la silla* = move the chair over. *Correrse* = to move one's self over: *córrase Ud. un poco, por favor* = please move over a little.

OBJECTION

objeción = "argument". This implies that the "objection" is based solely upon logical grounds: *hizo objeciones a mi religión* = he raised objections to my religion. Similarly with *objetar* = to raise (logical) objections.

inconveniente = "aversion". This implies a personal disadvantage or obstacle: *no veo inconveniente en que ella lo haga* = I see no objection in her doing it. Similarly with *oponerse a* = to object (be adverse) to.

OFFICE

oficina = this is a large office where many people work.

despacho = private office.

dirección = office of the director of an establishment. *(Dirección* is also the word for "address", especially in Spanish America.)

bufete = lawyer's office.

> NOTE: In some parts of Spanish America *(e.g.* Argentina) *estudio* is used.

consulta = doctor's office.

> NOTE: In Spanish America *consultorio* is usually preferred.

51

gabinete = dentist's office.

NOTE: In Spanish America *consultorio dental* (or *de dentista*) is generally used. See *gabinete* in PART I.

OLD

viejo This may refer to persons and things. When applied to persons it sometimes sounds harsh and disrespectful.

anciano This word is used exclusively in reference to persons, and is more auspicious than *viejo*. You can say *él es más viejo que ella* (he is older than she), or more idiomatically, *él tiene más años que ella,* but when referring to an aged person courtesy demands the use of *anciano*: an old man = *un anciano*.

antiguo Following a noun this adjective means "old" in the sense of "long standing": *un amigo antiguo* = an old friend (one which you have known for a long time); *una casa antigua* = an old house (one which has stood for many years, but not necessarily dilapidated). Placed before the noun it means either "former" or "ancient": *un antiguo profesor* = a former professor; *los antiguos romanos* = the ancient Romans.

ORDER

el orden = "order" in the sense of "arrangement": *todo está en orden* = everything is in order.

la orden = "order" in the sense of "command": *no entendí la orden* = I didn't understand the order.

pedido = "order" in the commercial sense. An "order for merchandise" should be translated as *un pedido* (or *una orden*) *de mercancías*.

52

pedir = "to order" in the sense of "request": *pedí la comida* = I ordered the dinner. *Encargar* may also be used but this implies that a certain amount of time must elapse before delivery can be made; it corresponds somewhat to the English "place an order": *he encargado tres toneladas de algodón* = I ordered three tons of cotton.

ordenar = "to order" in the sense of "command": *el oficial les ordenó que disparasen* = the officer ordered them to fire.

PART

This is usually rendered by *parte* (e.g. *tomar parte en* = to take part in, etc.) but observe the following departures:

hacer el papel = "to play (take) the part": *él hizo el papel del galán* = he took the part of the leading man.

pieza = "part of a machine" etc.: *piezas de recambio* (or *refacción)* = spare parts.

Note: In Mexico *piezas de repuesto* is used instead.

PLATFORM

The usual word is *plataforma*, but note the following special usages:

andén = railroad station platform.

programa político = platform of a political party.

POEM

poesía = short poem. This also means "poetry".

poema = a longer poem, approaching epic proportions: *el Poema de Mío Cid* = The Poem of the Cid.

POSSESSION

This can generally be translated by *poder,* and it is a common experience in commercial correspondence to find such

53

expressions as: *su carta está en mi poder* = I have your letter. *Posesión* should be avoided, for this is used almost exclusively in legal language where it means "disposition". Note that "to take possession" should be rendered *apoderarse de:* he took possession of the city = *se apoderó de la ciudad.*

PRISONER

prisionero = this is a military prisoner, a prisoner of war, and also some one captivated by affection and passion. A recent popular song in Cuba and Mexico was called *Prisionero del Mar,* a name which implies a certain romantic element as symbolized by *mar.*

preso = this is the more common word since it applies to civil prisoners: *el preso se escapó de la cárcel* = the prisoner escaped from jail.

PUT

poner = "to put" in a general and indefinite sense: *no recuerdo donde lo puse* = I don't remember where I put it. With *en* it indicates putting on the surface or the outside of something: *él puso la mano en mi hombro* = he put his hand on my shoulder.

NOTE: "To put on" (clothes) is *ponerse: se puso el traje* = he put on the suit. "To put on a hat" is often rendered by *cubrirse:* put on your hat! = *¡cúbrase!*

colocar = "to put with care and definite purpose", "to place": *colocó sus gafas en el bolsillo* = he put his glasses in his pocket.

meter = "to put in or into", "to insert": *ella metió las joyas en la caja* = she put the jewels in the box; *¡métase en lo que le importa!* = mind your own business!

54

NOTE: The idea of "put" is contained in certain verbs:
acostar = to put to bed
echar = to put out (of a place, position, etc.)

RATE

"Rate" (railroad, hotel, postage, etc.) is usually rendered *tarifa*, but note the following usages:
tipo de cambio = rate of exchange
tipo de interés = rate of interest
a razón de = at the rate of
a este paso = at this rate: *a este paso estaremos arrancados dentro de una semana* = at this rate we will be "broke" within a week.

REMAIN

permanecer = "to remain, stay". This verb implies the continuation of something which is already under way: *voy a permanecer hasta mañana* = I am going to stay until tomorrow.

quedar = "to remain, stay". This verb usually implies the initiation of something which is to continue: *fué a la Argentina, se quedó en Buenos Aires y permaneció allá cinco años* = he went to Argentina, stayed in Buenos Aires and remained there for five years.

See *leave*.

RETURN

regresar or *volver* = "to return" in the sense of "come or go back": *regresé a la Argentina* = I returned to Argentina.
devolver = "to return" in the sense of "give back": *devolví el libro* = I returned the book.

RIDE

ir a caballo = to ride on a horse (as a means of transportation)

ir en auto = to ride in an automobile *(i.e.* to go by car)

ir en tren = to ride in a train *(i.e.* to go by train)

ir en taxi = to ride in a taxi *(i.e.* to go by taxi)

montar a caballo = to ride horseback (as an accomplishment or for pleasure)

pasearse en auto = to take a ride in an automobile

pasearse en taxi = to take a ride in a taxi

See *drive* and *walk.*

SPEND

gastar dinero en = to spend money in (on)

pasar tiempo en = to spend time in (on)

llevar = "to spend time" in the sense of "to be ": *llevé dos años en Cuba* = I spent (was) two years in Cuba; *¿cuánto tiempo lleva Ud. en los Estados Unidos?* = how (long) much time have you spent (been) in the United States?

STAND

There is no equivalent for the English "to stand", so you should pay careful attention to the following renditions:

estar This is used for inanimate objects or for animate objects when the idea of "standing" is not emphasized: *la casa está en un cerro* = the house stands on a hill; *él estaba en un bosque* = he was standing in a forest.

estar (quedar) de pie = "to be standing". This is used when the idea of "standing" is to be clearly indicated, that is, in opposition to sitting or lying: *ella estaba de pie cuando entré* = she was standing (not sitting) when I came in.

mantenerse en pie = to remain standing

ponerse en pie = to stand up (said of persons)

alzarse = to stand up (said of animals)

sostenerse en pie = "to stand" when effort is involved: ***apenas***
    podía sostenerse en pie = he could hardly stand.

soportar = "to stand" in the sense of "endure" or "tolerate":
    no puedo soportarlo = I can't stand it.

STAY

See *remain*.

STILL

silencioso This means "still" in the sense of "quiet' : *¡esté*
    Ud. silencioso¡ = be still! *(i.e.* quiet).

quieto In spite of its appearance, this word does not mean
    "quiet" *(silencioso)*, but "still" in the sense of "motion-
    less": *¡esté Ud. quieto!* = stand still!

STOP

In translating the verb "to stop", you must distinguish between the transitive use *(e.g.* "to stop a person or thing")
and the intransitive use (not followed by a direct object).

detener This contains the idea of a temporary stop, **and**
    implies that the main action will be recontinued. When
    used intransitively, the reflexive form *detenerse* must be
    employed. Note the distinction: *se detuvo para dar un vis-
    tazo* = he stopped to take a look; *el freno detuvo el auto
    sólo un momento* = the brake stopped the car only **a**
    minute.

parar This implies that the main action has reached **its**
    intended end. The reflexive form *pararse* is not compulsory
    when used intransitively: *voy a parar(me) aquí mismo* =

I am going to stop right here; *él paró el motor* = **he** stopped the motor.

cesar de = "to cease, stop (doing something)". This is followed by the infinitive of another verb: *cesó de hablar* = he stopped talking.

dejar de = "to desist from", "to cut out" (colloquial). This is followed by either an infinitive or a noun: *¡deje de hablar!* = cut out the talking!; *¡déjese de tonterías!* = cut out the nonsense!

STRIKE

See *beat*.

pegar (or *dar) con* = "to strike with": *me pegó (dió) con el palo* = he struck me with the stick.

dar en = "to strike against": *la piedra dió en la ventana* = the stone struck the window.

dar de . . . en = "to strike (a part of the body) against": *dió de la cabeza en la pared* = he struck his head against the wall.

darle a uno un golpe = "to strike some one": *le dió un golpe al muchacho* = he struck (hit) the boy.

llamarle a uno la atención = "to strike one's attention": *eso es lo que me llamó la atención* = that is what struck my attention; *el ruido le llamó la atención a Juan* = the noise struck John's attention.

herirle a una (la vista, los oídos) = "to strike one's eyes, ears: *un sonido extraño me hirió los oídos* = a strange sound struck my ears; *la luz le hirió la vista a Juan* = the light struck John's eyes.

NOTE: A "strike" in the sense of a body of employees quitting work, is *huelga* in Spanish.

58

TAKE

llevar = "to take" in the sense of "carry". This word should
always be used when "to take to a place" is meant: *llevé
la carta a la casa de correos* = I took the letter to the
post office.

llevarse = "to take away". This verb does not indicate any
particular destination, but merely stresses the idea of removal: *el criado se llevó los platos* = the servant took
away the plates.

tomar This verb has a less definite meaning; it merely indicates that the subject has acquired or "taken to himself"
the object in question. There is no indication of carrying,
destination or removal: *él tomó mi libro* = he took my
book; *voy a tomar un tren* = I am going to take a train;
tomar a broma = to take as a joke; *tomar sobre sí* = to
take upon one's self.

> NOTE: *Tomar* translates "to drink" and "to eat":
> *nunca tomo sopa* = I never eat soup; *¿quiere Ud.
> tomar un refresco?* = would you like to have a (soft)
> drink?

quitar a = "to take away". This verb indicates separation:
me quitó el libro = he took the book away from me; *le
quité el libro a Juan* = I took the book away from John.
Note that Spanish uses *a* ("to") where English uses "from"
(this is the so-called "dative of separation"). Also note
that *quitarse* means "to take off", "to undress": *se quitó
la ropa* = he took off his clothes.

Many verbs contain the idea of English "take":

cuidar de = to take care
encargarse de = to take charge of
sacar = to take out

salir a = to take after (i.e. resemble)
aprovecharse de = to take advantage of
tener gusto en = to take pleasure in
correr el riesgo = to take a chance
despedirse de = to take leave of
hacer un viaje = to take a trip
dar un paseo = to take a walk
darse cuenta de = to take into consideration
caer enfermo = to take sick
tardar (demorarse) en = to take time in
guardarse de = to take care not to: *guárdese de caer* = be careful not to fall.

NOTE: When purchasing something in a store, "I'll take this" is expressed *Me quedo con éste.*

THERE

The words for "here" and "there" vary according to whether rest or motion is implied, and to the amount of distance indicated. These differences are usually maintained and you should master them at the outset.

rest	motion	
aquí	acá	here (near the speaker)
ahí	ahí	there (near person spoken to)
allí	allá	there (distant from both persons)

NOTE: The only exception is in the use of *allá.* It is obligatory when followed by *en* and the name of a place, despite the fact that no motion is indicated in such cases: *allá en el Rancho Grande* (do you remember this Mexican song?) = out there on the Big Ranch.

THROW

echar = this verb implies a minimum of effort and calls attention to the object or its destination. Thus it corresponds

60

somewhat to the English "cast", or "toss": *echó el abrigo sobre la silla* = he tossed his overcoat on the chair.

tirar = the usual meaning of English "throw". A few years back during the revolutionary period in Cuba there was a popular song called *¿Quién tiró la Bomba?* = Who Threw the Bomb?

> NOTE: In Colombia and sporadically elsewhere, it is advisable to avoid this verb, since it has acquired another meaning which is socially tabu. See introductory "A Word to the Wise".

arrojar = "to hurl". This implies forceful and violent action, accompanied in most cases by emotion: *arrojó el cuadro contra la pared* = he hurled the picture against the wall.

UNDERSTAND

entender This verb implies the responsibility for comprehension rests with the speaker: *no le entiendo* = I don't understand you (because I can't hear you, I am incapable of understanding your speech).

comprender This verb implies the responsibility for comprehension rests with the person addressed: *no le comprendo* = I don't understand you (because you speak obscurely, you use difficult language).

With *entender* the speaker is at fault, with *comprender* the listener is at fault. This distinction is significant, for its neglect may possibly imply a slight.

WALK

See *drive* and *ride*.

caminar = "to walk" as a means of locomotion or travel.

ir a pie = "to walk" in opposition to riding.

61

dar un paseo (or *una vuelta*) = to take a walk (for exercise or pleasure).
ir a pasearse (or *ir a paseo*) = to go out for a walk.
pasearse = "to walk" for pleasure or diversion.

WORD

"Word" is almost always *palabra*. In linguistic literature and etymological dictionaries you will often find *voz* and *vocablo*, which correspond to the English "term". Note carefully that "words of a song" must be expressed by *letra*: I don't know the words to that song = *no sé la letra de esa canción*.

WORKER

trabajador = One who does any kind of work, either mental or physical. This is the general term.
operario = "skilled worker", usually mechanical. This is the worker with a craft or special trade.
obrero = "laborer"; manual worker without any necessary skill or specialized craft. As a general term it means the "workingman" as contrasted to the "white collar" class.
jornalero = day laborer or journeyman. This worker is hired by the day.
peón = "hired hand"; this is the lowest kind of worker. He is usually found in rural areas doing farm labor.

III. FORGET YOUR ENGLISH!

THIS IS intended to take you a step further into the psychology of the Spanish language. One of the greatest obstacles in the learning of any foreign language is to replace the language habits of English with those of the new language. Many students learn to speak with comparative fluency and with a good accent, but what they say is simply not "Spanish". They have missed one of the most important and elusive features, that is, the Spanish point of view. Your Spanish will never be natural until you have acquired the Spanish way of saying things. This section is designed to give you some hints on how this may be done, by indicating some common failings and by supplanting these with useful insights into Spanish psychology.

(1) *Literal Translations*

One of the most flagrant pitfalls for students is the literal translation of English constructions and idioms into Spanish. Such errors will mark the novice more quickly than those discussed in PARTS I and II. Take special precautions to avoid such egregious translations as the following:

DO NOT SAY: (when smoking)

Déme luz for "give me a light". Do you realize what this means? *Dar a luz* means either "to give birth" or "to publish". Avoid ridicule by saying: *Déme lumbre*.

DO NOT SAY: (in a restaurant)

¿Tiene Ud. leche? for "do you have any milk?" The waitress

would surely blush, for this refers to a flow of milk. By all means say: *¿Hay leche?*

Café negro for "black coffee". You are apt to get something for which you did not bargain if you say this. The proper expression is *café puro* or *café solo*.

NOTE: In Colombia *café tinto*.

Spanish, unlike English, does not like to form compound words. So avoid such things as *leche muchacha* for "milk-maid" *(lechera)*, *vaca muchacho* for "cowboy" *(vaquero)*. The following are among the most important legitimate compound words:

el sobretodo = the overcoat *el ferrocarril* = the railroad *el pasatiempo* = the pastime	form their plurals according to normal rules
el rascacielos = the skyscraper *el paraguas* = the umbrella *el parabrisas* = the windshield *el portamonedas* = the purse *el cortaplumas* = the penknife *el limpiabotas* = the bootblack	remain unchanged in the plural
el quehacer = the duty, chore, task *el vaivén* = the moving, coming and going *el hazmerreír* = the laughing stock, funny person	rarely used in the plural

boquiabierto = open-mouthed, gaping
carilargo = long-faced
ojinegro = black-eyed
pelirrubio = light-haired

(2) *Spanish Patterns of Expression*

A feature which will immediately make your Spanish more

64

"native" is the casting of your thoughts in certain patterns of expression which are typically Spanish. The following represents a crystallization of some of the most common patterns. Try to acquire the "feeling" of these patterns and use the accompanying models as a guide for all similar sentences.

(a) *Claro (seguro) que* + *indicative* = Of course + indicative:

> *Claro que hablo español* = Of course I speak Spanish
> *Claro que sí* = Yes, of course
> *Claro que no* = Of course not
> *¡Claro está!* = Of course!

(b) *Sí (que)* + *indicative* = certainly (indeed) + indicative. *Sí* is used to emphasize an assertion. Sometimes it is followed by *que*, and is generally equivalent to the English emphatic auxiliary "do" or the expletive "indeed":

> *¡Sí que no sabe nada!* = He certainly doesn't know anything!
> *¡Sí que vengo!* = Certainly I'm coming!
> *¡Sí que sí!* = Yes indeed!
> *¡Sí que no!* = Certainly not!
> *¡Eso sí que es!* = *That*'s it!
> *¡Eso sí que es lo que quiero!* = *That*'s what I want!
> *¡Ahora sí lo creo!* = Now I *do* believe it!
> *¡Eso sí que es bueno!* = That is indeed good!
> *¡Sí que lo hará!* = Certainly he will do it!

(c) *Si* + *indicative* = Why + indicative

Used in this way *si* indicates surprise. It is often preceded by *pero*.

> *¡Si no sabe nada!* = Why, he doesn't know anything!
> *¡Si no lo creo!* = Why, I don't believe it!
> *¡Vaya si pasó!* = I should say something happened!

¡Vaya si es verdad! = I should say it's true!

¡Pero si ya lo tiene! = Why, you already have it!

¡Pero apenas si ví nada! = Why, I hardly saw a thing!

(d) *A (para) qué* + *infinitive* = What's the good of + present participle:

    ¿A (para) qué hacer eso? = What's the good of doing that?

(e) *A que* + *indicative*[1] = I'll bet (that) + indicative:

    A que no sabe = I'll bet you don't know

    A que no = I'll bet not; I'll bet you can't, etc.

    A que sí = I'll bet it is; I'll bet I can, etc.

(f) *Lo cierto es que* + *indicative* = As a matter of fact; in fact + indicative:

    Lo cierto es que no lo tengo = As a matter of fact I don't have it.

    Lo cierto es que no sé = In fact I don't know.

(g) *La verdad es que* + *indicative* = Really + indicative:

    La verdad es que no vale la pena = It's really not worth the trouble.

    La verdad es que no entiendo = I really don't understand.

(h) *¿Qué hay de . . . ?* = What about . . . ?

    ¿Qué hay de mí? = What about me?

    ¿Qué hay de los niños? = What about the children?

(i) *Es que . . .* = It (that) is because. Well, . . .

This pattern is used to explain a previous remark. In English it is frequently left unexpressed or rendered by "well":

    — *Ud. parece muy cansado.* (You look very tired)

    — *Es que no he dormido.* (Well, I haven't slept)

---

[1] In this pattern, *apuesto* ("bet") is understood, and sometimes even expressed: *Apuesto a que no sabe,* etc.

66

— *Él habla español perfectamente.* (He speaks Spanish perfectly.)

— *Es que pasó mucho tiempo en Méjico.* (Well, he spent a lot of time in Mexico.)

(j) *A propósito de . . .* = Speaking of . . .

A propósito de viajes, me voy a Cuba = Speaking of trips, I am going to Cuba.

(k) *De ahí que + indicative* = So that's why + indicative.

This pattern indicates that something which has just been said explains that which is about to be said (following *De ahí que*):

De ahí que·me encuentra tan ocupado = So that's why you find me so busy.

De ahí que vine a la Argentina = And that's why I came to Argentina.

(l) *Cómo no + haber de + infinitive* = Of course, why shouldn't + indicative.

This pattern is used to remove an element of doubt in a previous statement or question:

— *¿Ud. entiende lo que digo?* (Do you understand what I say?)

— *¡Cómo no he de entender!* (Of course, why shouldn't I understand!)

(m) *Cómo que no + indicative* = Why, certainly + indicative.

This pattern indicates a contradiction of a previous statement:

— *Ud. no ha estudiado la lección.* (You haven't studied the lesson.)

— *¡Cómo que no he estudiado la lección!* (Why, certainly I have!)

67

(3) *Expletives*

It will make your Spanish more idiomatic if from time to time you judiciously punctuate your conversation with the following:

Ahora bien = Now then,
Pues bien = Well then,
¡Pues qué! = Well, what about it!, So what?
¡Y qué! = What! (expressing amazement)
Vaya pues = Well
¡Vaya! = Well now!
¿Y pues? = So? How is that?
Pues sí = Yes indeed
Pues no = Not at all
¡Deja! = Never mind!
Digo . . . = I mean . . . (said when amplifying or correcting a previous statement)
¡Oiga! = Listen! Say!
Eso es = That's right (expressing agreement)
Es decir . . . = That is to say . . .
Bueno = All right; O.K.

(4) *Hints on Word Order*

(a) Do not separate the two verb forms of a compound tense:
¿Ha escrito Ud. la carta? = Have you written the letter?
Not: *¿Ha Ud. escrito la carta?*

(b) When both the subject and the predicate (direct object or predicate adjectives) follow the verb, the shorter is placed first:
¿Es fácil la lección? (Is the lesson easy?)
¿Es la lección fácil o difícil? (Is the lesson easy or difficult?)

68

¿Compró la casa su señor padre? (Did your father buy the house?)

¿Compró su padre todas estas casas? (Did your father buy all these houses?)

(c) In subordinate clauses, the subject often follows the verb if there is no noun object:

Espere hasta que llegue el tren. (Wait until the train arrives.) Not: *Espere hasta que el tren llegue.*

(5) *The Use of YA*

Ya has various shades of meaning depending upon the tense of the verb. The translation "already" is deceiving and in many cases inaccurate. Note that *ya* usually stands at the beginning of the sentence:

(a) *Present Tense:* "now", "already". Often it merely adds emphasis to the main assertion.

Ya voy = I'm coming right away

Ya lo creo = I should say so!

Ya se ve = You can see; It's obvious

Ya lo ve = You can see for yourself; There you are!

¡Ya caigo! = Now I get (understand) it!

¡Ya sé! = I know!

¡Ya lo sé! = Of course!

Ahí están ya = There they are now

Ya sabe Ud. = You surely know

Ya eso es otra cosa = Now that's a very different thing.

Ya pasa de las doce = It's after twelve o'clock

Ya recuerdo = I *do* recall

Ya es la hora = Now is the time; The time has come; It's time

¿Me entiende Ud. ya? = Do you understand me now?

69

¡Ya está hecho! = There, that's done!

Ya llega el tren = The train is arriving now

Ya es tarde = It's late now

¡Ya está claro! = It's obvious!

(b) *Future Tense:* "soon", "presently", "in due time".

Ya se hará eso = That will be done presently.

Ya lo haré = I'll do it in time.

Ya volverá = He'll come back soon

Ya lo haré más tarde = I'll do it later on

(c) *Past Tenses:* "some time ago", "already".

Although the preterite tense is usually used in such cases, note that it corresponds to the present perfect (compound with "have") of English:

Ya acabé = I have already finished

Ya lo ví = I have already seen it

¡Ya pasó! = It's all over with!

Ya se acabó = It's finished

(d) *Imperfect Tense: ya* intensifies the assertion.

¡Ya me lo esperaba yo! = I was *expecting* it!

¡Ya me lo temía yo! = I was *afraid* of that!

¡Ya lo decía yo! = Didn't I *say* so! I was *sure* of it!

(e) Note the following:

ya no = no longer, no more, not now

no ya = not only

ya que = since, because, now that

¡ya ya! = yes yes! all right, all right!

(6) Adjectives With Variable Meanings

(a) Many adjectives have different meanings depending upon whether they are used with *ser* or *estar*. In accordance with the general rule, you will note that with *ser* they denote a

70

characteristic which is inherent and habitual, while with *estar* they denote only temporary conditions.

	with SER	*With ESTAR*
bueno	good (of character)	well (health), good (food)
malo	bad (of character)	ill
callado	taciturn	silent, quiet (of persons)
borracho	drunkard	drunk
loco	insane	furious
cansado	tiresome, boring	tired
divertido	amusing	amused
alegre	gay, merry (in nature)	glad
rico	rich (of persons)	wealthy, delicious (of food)
pálido	pale in complexion	temporarily pale
joven	young in years	young in appearance
cierto	true	sure, certain
pensativo	thoughtful (by nature)	pensive (at the time)
amable	amiable	in an amiable mood

For *cómodo* see COMFORTABLE in Part II.

When in doubt as to use *ser* or *estar* with a predicate adjective, you will often be safe to employ *quedar: quedó pensativo* = he was (remained) pensive.

(b) A number of adjectives vary in meaning depending upon whether they precede or follow the noun. When following the noun, adjectives usually have a literal or commonplace meaning, and serve to distinguish a particular kind of the object from another. Adjectives of color, nationality, and physical qualities almost always follow the noun. Placed

71

before the noun, adjectives lose much of their force and often imply a figurative or poetic meaning. As such they denote qualities which are inherent in the object in general and do not distinguish one kind of the object from another.

It is well to remember that the word which comes last assumes the chief importance, whether it be the adjective or the noun. In cases of doubt, you will usually be safe in placing the adjective last.

	Before the Noun	*After the Noun*
bueno	good (fine, likeable)	good (in character)
pobre	poor (to be pitied)	poor (without money)
nuevo	new (different), other	(brand-) new
gran(de)	great	large, tall
mismo	same	(him, your, etc.) -self the very, even
diferentes	several	different
varios	several	various, different
cierto	a certain	authentic, reliable
propio	(his, your, etc.) own	(him, your, etc.) -self
antiguo	ancient, former	of long standing
caro	dear	expensive
simple	single, simple	foolish, artless
puro	mere, sheer, absolute	pure

(7) *Some Verbal Oddities*

(a) Certain every-day verbs change in meaning according to the tense in which they are used.

saber: imperfect = "knew": *yo lo sabía* = I knew it.

preterite = "found out": *lo supe* = I found it out.

conocer: imperfect = "knew" (was acquainted with): *le conocía* = I knew him.

72

preterite = "met" (got to know): *le conocí* = I met (got to know) him.

tener: imperfect = "had": *yo tenía una carta* = I had (possessed) a letter.

preterite = "received": *tuve una carta* = I had (received) a letter.

ser: imperfect = "was, were": *él era mi maestro* = he was my teacher.

preterite = "became": *él fué mi maestro* = he became my teacher.

querer: imperfect = "wanted": *yo quería hacerlo* = I wanted to do it.

preterite = "tried": *yo quise hacerlo* = I tried to do it.

(b) Be especially careful with the verb *querer*. It has an entirely different meaning when followed by *a:*

Quiero una criada. = I *want* a servant girl.

Quiero a una criada. = I *love* a servant girl.

(c) *Pagar:* "for" *(por)* is usually not translated unless both the price and the object bought are mentioned. The person paid is always the indirect object.

Pagué el traje al sastre. = I paid the tailor for the suit.

but —

Pagué al sastre cuarenta pesos por el traje. = I paid the tailor forty pesos for the suit.

(d) *Muerto*, the past participle of *morir*, not only means "dead" and "died", but also "killed". In the last case it is not as ill-sounding as *matado* (from *matar*, "to kill"), which is generally confined to the killing of animals, suicide and figurative uses.

Haber muerto = To have died

Haber muerto + *direct object* = To have killed (a person)

Ser muerto = To be killed

Estar muerto = To be dead

(e) With the verbs *comprar* (to buy), *quitar* (to take away), *robar* (to rob), *tomar* (to take), *conseguir* (to get), the English "from" is rendered by *a* ("to") in Spanish:

Me robó el dinero = He stole the money from me

Ella se lo compró a él = She bought it from him

Se lo conseguí a ellos = I got it from them

Me quita el sueño = It deprives me of sleep *(i.e.* It keeps me from sleeping.)

(8) *Modes of Address*

CABALLERO, SEÑOR

Caballero is more formal than *señor*, but is less respectful, and therefore is not used by servants and other inferiors when speaking to superiors. *Caballero* is used only between equals and cannot be followed by the man's name. It is somewhat more frequent in Spanish America than in Spain.

DON, DOÑA

These are titles of respect which are followed by the person's first name, with or without the last name. Note that *doña* is used for both married and unmarried women. It is somewhat more eloquent (and definite) to include the last name. It is even more formal to precede *don* and *doña* with *señor*, *señora* and *señorita*, in which case the last name must be used and a distinction between married and unmarried women can be made. Thus an unmarried lady may be known as:

Señorita González
Doña Laura (González)
Srta. Doña Laura González

In Spain it is usual to speak of persons by using *don* and *doña* followed by the first name, this being somewhat less formal than *señor, señora* and *señorita* and the last name. In Spanish America, however, *don* and *doña* are more formal and eloquent, and *señor* etc. followed by the last name is preferred.

MUJER, ESPOSA, SEÑORA

Normally when speaking of one's wife, one says *mi mujer*. Politeness may be had by using *mi esposa* or *mi señora* (less usual). When speaking of the wife of another, *su señora* must be used. When speaking to one's wife a man generally says *mujer*. In speaking to a woman, it is also common to punctuate one's speech with an occasional exclamatory *¡mujer!*, whether she be your wife or not.

HOMBRE, MARIDO, ESPOSO, SEÑOR

As an exclamation *¡hombre!* corresponds to the English "man alive!", and may be used in speaking to either men or women. In speaking of her husband or that of someone else, a woman generally says *marido* or more formally, *esposo. Hombre* cannot be used to mean "husband", nor can *señor* (except humorously) which in such cases would mean "master". Note that "husband and wife" is rendered *esposos* or *matrimonio* in Spanish. When spelled with a capital, *Señor* means "Lord" (God).

75

USTED, TÚ, VOSOTROS, VOS

A good plan is always to use *usted* until the other person initiates the use of *tú*. It is often difficult for an American to know just when *tú* is appropriate, and it is therefore best to let the responsibility rest with your Spanish friends. In this way you run no risk of being injudiciously familiar. Although *usted* is ordinarily expressed for politeness, it should not be repeated too often. To use it once in a sentence is quite sufficient, unless, of course, your meaning would otherwise be obscure. Constant repetition of *usted* sometimes indicates anger, contempt, etc., so take care!

You will probably never have an occasion to use *vosotros*. In Spain it is employed as the plural of *tú*. In Spanish America, however, this practice has fallen into disuse and *ustedes* is heard instead. Thus a Spanish American parent who called his son and daughter singly by *tú*, would address them collectively by *ustedes*. In Spanish America *vosotros* is reserved for eloquent and oratorical effects.

In the familiar language of most of Central America, in the low-class speech of many places in South America, and quite generally in Argentina and Uruguay, *tú* is replaced by the archaic *vos*. The use of *vos* is virtually unknown, however, in Peru, Bolivia, Mexico and the Antilles. The verb endings for *vos* vary somewhat from place to place, but the most usual (Argentina, Central America) may be glimpsed from the forms: *tenés* (tienes), *hablás* (hablas), *escribís* (escribes). Elsewhere the same endings as the second plural are used, and in some parts (Ecuador, Colombia, Venezuela, etc.) both systems are found side by side. Except for the River Plate area and perhaps Central America where this usage is almost universal in familiar language, you are advised to avoid *vos*.

(9) *Spanish Personal Names*

A point which is neglected with amazing frequency is the matter of Spanish names. At first glance these seem highly bewildering, but the complexities are for the most part only apparent. To the Spaniard, as to everyone else, the sound of his own name is one of the most gratifying and important sounds in the whole language. Therefore, any neglect of this matter would not only be very inauspicious for the student of Spanish, but would also brand you as a socially inept *gringo*.

In Spanish a person has two "last names". Take for example, *Juan Díaz y Durán*. *Díaz* is the family name of his father and *Durán* is the family name of his mother *(i.e.* her "maiden name"). Only *Díaz*, however, serves as his family name and continues down through the generations of the family. The mother's name of course, would change from generation to generation. It is placed after the father's family name and is usually (but not always) connected to it by *y*.

Arturo *Díaz* y Núñez (father) ⎫
Ana *Durán* y Silva (mother) ⎬ Juan Díaz y Durán

The name of an unmarried woman has the same construction, except that *de* is often placed before the name of her father:[1]

Pedro *López* y Martínez (father) ⎫
Lola *Gómez* y Blasco (mother) ⎬ María (de) López y Gómez

Now say that *María de López y Gómez* marries *Juan Díaz y Durán*. Her name would then become *María López de Díaz*. Note that *de* is then placed before the name of her husband. It is convenient to remember that *de* serves to indicate to "whom" the woman "belongs". On marriage, a woman usual-

---

[1] The insertion of the *de* is more frequent in Spain than Spanish America.

ly drops the family name of her mother, although in some cases she may choose to retain it: *María López de Díaz y Gómez*.

The children of this union might possibly be:

Juan *Díaz* y Durán   María (de) *López* y Gómez (mother
    (father)   (Married name: María López de Díaz)

        José Díaz y López (son)
        Luisa (de) Díaz y López (daughter)

Note carefully that a person can never be addressed by his mother's family name alone. In the above case, you may say either *Señor Díaz* or *Señor Díaz y Durán*. The mother's family name is often abbreviated to a single initial: *Juan Díaz D.* When going to a foreign country where the complexities of Spanish names are not understood, a Spaniard will usually drop his mother's name altogether, since it appears last and might cause him to be addressed by it alone.

Family names are never pluralized as in English: *Los Loja* = the Lojas; *Los López* = the López family. Foreign names are treated in the same manner: *Los Smith* = the Smiths.

(10) *Spanish Social Customs*

The successful acquisition of a foreign language entails not only a change of language habits but also a variation of social behavior. This is even more important in Spanish than in most languages because of the great number of expressions and formulas reflecting underlying social attitudes and customs.

This applies to Spanish wherever it may be spoken, although peninsular Spaniards are perhaps somewhat more partial to such amenities than are Spanish Americans. It goes without

78

saying then, that you should try to use such expressions as *muchas gracias* ("many thanks"), *de nada* ("it's nothing at all"), *con mucho gusto* ("with the greatest of pleasure"), *Ud. es muy amable* ("you are very kind"), and *a sus órdenes* ("at your service") at the slightest provocation.

(a) GREETINGS

Adiós: means "hello" *(hola)* as well as "good-bye".
Buenos días: used all morning.
Buenas tardes: used from noon to sundown.
Buenas noches: used after sundown on greeting as well as on taking leave.

These can be made more friendly and personal by reinforcing them with *muy:*

— *Muy buenas noches, Tomás.*

The usual reply will simply be:

— *Muy buenas, Alberto.*

A general inquiry as to health, affairs, etc.:

¿Cómo le va?	
¿Cómo lo pasa Ud.?	
¿Cómo sigue Ud.?	How is it going?
¿Qué pasa? (In Mexico = *¿Qué pasó?*)	What's new?
	How are things?
¿Qué hubo?[1] (In Mexico = *¿Qué húbole?*; in Cuba = *¿Qué cuenta?*)	

In reply you say:

Regular	So, so.
Así, así (In many parts of Spanish America = *así no más*)	Middling well.

---

[1] Usually pronounced as if written *quiúbo* (kyooboh).

Or:

Voy pasando
Pasándolo (In Mexico=*pasándola*) ⎱ I manage to
Voy tirando ⎰ get by.

Or:

Muy bien = Very well
Perfectamente = Fine
Mejor que nunca = Never better
Lo de siempre = The same as usual

(b) LEAVE-TAKING

Adiós (in the familiar speech of
   Argentina and Chile = *¡Chao!*) ⎱ Good-bye.
¡Que lo pase bien! ⎰

Hasta la vista ⎫ These expressions
Hasta luego (lueguito and *lueguecito* ⎪ imply that you
   are common in Spanish America) ⎬ will meet again
Nos vemos or *nos veremos* (Mexican) ⎭ soon.

¡Vaya con Dios! — said by the one who remains to the
   one who is leaving.

¡Quede con Dios! — said by the one who is leaving to
   the one who remains.

(c) ADMIRATION

When you happen to admire something belonging to another
person, he will offer it to you, saying such things as:

(Está) a su disposición.
Es suyo.
Lo tiene a sus órdenes.

80

But such offers are only empty formalities and you are expected to decline them by replying:

Está muy bien empleado.

Está en buenas manos.

No podría mejorar de dueño.

(d) EATING AND DINING

When partaking of food or drink it is customary to offer some to those who may be present, whether you are acquainted with them or not:

¿Le gusta?

¿Ud. quiere?

This offer is expected to be declined (unless persisted in) by saying:

Muchas gracias. ¡Que aproveche! (or: *¡Buen provecho!)*

When sitting down to dine, you should greet those already present by saying *buenos días, buenas tardes* or *buenas noches,* depending on the time of day (see GREETINGS above). When leaving the table you should say to those still seated:

¡Buen provecho! (or: *¡Que aprovechen!*)

(e) PERMISSION

The matter of requesting permission is very important in Spanish. When entering the room, office, etc. of another person it is always best to inquire:

¿Se puede?

Con (su) permiso (or: *con su venia)*

The answer will usually be: *¡No faltaba más!* or *Ud. es muy dueño,* or a mere nod of assent.

When excusing yourself for something which you are about to do, such as leaving the room, table, interrupting,

81

turning your attention to something else in the presence of another person, etc., it is necessary to say *con (su) permiso* (see EXCUSE ME in *Part II*). The answer to this request is the same as above.

(f) INTRODUCTIONS

When you wish to introduce one person to another, say:

Permítame (or: *Tengo el gusto de) presentarle a mi amigo* = Permit me (I have the pleasure) to introduce to you my friend.

The first person to acknowledge the introduction will answer:

Tanto (or: *Mucho) gusto en conocerle.*

The second person will then reply:

El gusto es mío.

(g) IDENTIFYING ONE'S SELF

When introducing yourself, or when giving your name, profession, nationality, etc., it is polite to add *a sus órdenes* or *para servirle:*

— *¿Cómo se llama Ud.?*

— *Juan Gómez, a sus órdenes* (or: *para servirle).*

The phrase *a sus órdenes* is in constant use when it is desired to indicate to another person that you are anxious to be compliant and amenable:

— *¿Puedo verle alguna vez sobre este asunto?*

— *¡Sí señor! A sus órdenes.*

When mentioning your address it is polite to add: *donde tiene su casa,* or *a su disposición:*

— *¿Dónde vive Ud.?*

— *San Rafael, número 1005, donde tiene su casa* (or: *a su disposición).*

The other person will reply:

Y la suya está . . .

Or if it is supposed that you already know his address, he will merely add:

Ya sabe Ud. donde tiene su casa.

It must be born in mind that such remarks, unless further specified, do not constitute an invitation to call.

(h) VISITING

When receiving a visitor it is customary to offer him your house, saying:

Aquí Ud. tiene su casa.

Or more formally:

Ud. ha tomado posesión de su casa.

When taking leave from a visit, you should say:

Yo no molesto más. Si no manda Ud. otra cosa, me despido.

— and decline any attempts of your host to see you to the door:

No se moleste (en acompañarme).

but he will probably do so anyway, replying:

No es molestia ninguna. Ya sabe Ud. donde tiene su casa.

(i) ON THE TELEPHONE

In answering the telephone, "hello" is rendered differently according to the country:

¡Diga! (Spain)
¡Bueno! (Mexico)
¡Aló! (Peru and Ecuador)
¡A ver! (Colombia)
¡Hola! (Argentina, Uruguay, and most other places)
¿Qué hay? (Cuba)

Note the following usages:

$\left.\begin{array}{l}\textit{¿Quién habla?}\\ \textit{¿Con quién hablo?}\\ \textit{¿Qué casa es ésa?}\ \text{(Cuba)}\end{array}\right\}$ Who is speaking?

¿Está el señor Gómez? = Is Mr. Gomez there?

Dígale a Juan que se ponga al aparato = Tell John to come to the 'phone

Con él (Juan) habla = This is he (John)

¿De parte de quién? = Who shall I say is calling?[1]

De parte de Alberto = You may say that Alberto is calling[1]

Le llaman al aparato = You're wanted on the telephone

(11) *Some Hints on Pronunciation*

Forgetting your English habits of pronunciation is highly essential if your Spanish is not to offend native listeners. The complete eradication of the English accent involves many subtle distinctions which can be appreciated only after considerable training or prolonged exposure to the speech of natives.

However, a large part of the bad accents heard among Americans can be directly attributed to certain rather elementary oversights, which, despite their simplicity and general recognition, are a constant object of neglect. It is the disregard for these same points that grates so offensively on Spanish ears. Consequently, you will do yourself a great favor by carefully attending to the following:

Literally, the phrase *de parte de* means "in behalf of". It is used in making and answering inquiries for the benefit of a third person. For instance, if you wish to see Sr. Campos at his office, his secretary will ask: *¿De parte de quién?* — and you must answer: *De parte del Sr. + your name.* The same applies to social visits, etc.

VOWELS: The vowels of Spanish are not drawled or prolonged as in English; in fact, the Spanish vowel requires about one-half less time to enunciate than does the average English vowel. It is this feature which gives spoken Spanish its "machine gun" like quality. You should therefore try to pronounce Spanish words quickly and crisply, but clearly and without "slurring". The Spanish *tú*, for instance, sounds quite different from the English *to*. In the Spanish word, the "oo" sound is very short and precise; in the English word the vowel is prolonged, and lacks forceful articulation.

In English there is also a marked tendency to pronounce clearly only the accented vowel in a word, and to "slur" the remaining vowels into a sound something like the *a* in "about". This is particularly distasteful to Spanish ears. In Spanish each vowel must always be given the same full sound regardless of position or accent. For example, in the English word "capital", only the first *a* is clearly articulated: *ca'-puh-tuhl*. In the Spanish word, *capital*, each vowel is distinctly sounded: *cah-pee-tahl'*. Do not say *uhn-tohn'-suhs* for *entonces;* sound each vowel clearly: *en-tohn'-sehs*.

d Do not pronounce this as the *d* in "day" except when following a pause in breath[1] or the letters *l* and *n: Donde, caldo, senda*. Otherwise *d* is like the *th* in "though": *lado, arder, desdén, dado*. To pronounce the latter words with the *d* of "day" is very confusing to the Spaniard, for in such cases the English *d* sounds like the Spanish *r*. Thus *cada* is mistaken for *cara*, etc.

---

[1] A pause in breath normally occurs before the beginning of each sentence, although it may occur within a sentence before a word which is to be emphasized.

NOTE: At the end of a word and in the past participle ending *–ado, d* is pronounced very lightly, that is, the tip of the tongue barely touches the teeth. Many speakers omit this sound altogether in colloquial speech, saying *hablao* for *hablado,* and *ciudá* for *ciudad.* This occurs principally in the coastal regions of South America, quite generally in Cuba, Puerto Rico and the Dominican Republic, along the Gulf coast of Mexico, and among certain Spaniards. Practically everyone drops the *d* in *usted (= usté).* But to omit *d* in other than these aforementioned cases is considered vulgar and indicates a lack of education.

b, v These two letters are pronounced exactly alike in Spanish, the sound depending upon their position in a word:

(1) after a pause in breath or the letters *m, n,* the sound is like the *b* in "boy": *invidia, en verano, en Barcelona, embajada.*

(2) in all other positions they have a sound peculiar to Spanish. It is produced by saying the *b* in "boy" without the lips actually touching, so that the breath may escape: *es bobo, me voy, la vida, escribir, lavar.*

To the English ear, this sound appears at times like the English *b* and at other times like the English *v.*

NOTE: The sound of English *v* does not occur in correct Spanish. It does, however, occur in the speech of a few persons who have a tendency toward affectation, and among certain Spaniards who are influenced by local languages (such as Basque and Catalán). Since the English *v* is regarded as either affected or vulgar, you should by all means avoid it and cultivate the proper Spanish sound.

r This sound is often difficult for Americans to acquire. For certain Englishmen, however, the sound in quite natural since they normally use it in such words as "very" and "sorry". American humor transcribes such pronunciations as "veddy" and "soddy", because the *r* sounds very much like the *dd* in "ladder" when said quickly. The Spanish (and British) sound consists of a single flip of the tongue against the roots of the upper front teeth. If you use the rapid *dd* of the English "ladder", you will approximate the Spanish sound much more closely than if you use the American *r*.

rr The Spanish *rr* is the above sound produced three (usually) times in rapid succession. This is the so-called "trilled" *r*. It represents not only the doubled *r*, but also the single *r* when initial or following the letters *n* and *l*: *carro, rio, Enrique, alrededor*. This sound should be carefully distinguished from the single "flipped" *r* described immediately above, for in some cases the meanings of words vary: *caro – carro; pero – perro*.

(12) *Differences Between Spanish America and Spain*

You are undoubtedly aware that there are differences between the pronunciation of Spanish America and the Castilian pronunciation of Spain.[1] It is therefore quite natural to ask: Which pronunciation should I use? Actually, both are equally correct; it all depends upon where you are from and with

---

[1] Castilian Spanish is the standard language of Spain, and is based upon that speech pattern heard in the north-central part (province of Castile).

whom you intend to deal. Things to be avoided are: (1) vacillation between the two pronunciations, (2) features which are considered vulgar in both Spanish America and Spain. The best rule is to choose one system of pronunciation and then stick to it! Which system you choose will be determined by your purposes in wanting to speak Spanish.

On the whole, the Castilian pronunciation is not well received in Spanish America. It is considered "foreign", and sounds pedantic and overly affected. The person with a Castilian accent is apt to be branded *gallego* — a term which means "Galician" (a native of the Spanish province of Galicia), but which many Spanish Americans apply contemptuously to all Spaniards.[1] Thus if your interests fall south of the border, by all means do not adopt the Castilian pronunciation. On the other hand, if you are exclusively inclined toward Spain and its literature, the Castilian offers the only proper pronunciation.

Should you decide in favor of the Spanish American manner, you must realize that the Spanish American pronunciation itself varies from place to place. There is no single Spanish American "pronunciation" — there are "pronunciations". Such finer points, however, need not concern you, since your intention should simply be to acquire an accent which will sound natural to the average Spanish American.

The following points of difference will suffice to bring out a practical distinction between the pronunciation of Castilian and American Spanish:

c, z, s, In northern Spain, the letters *c* (before *e* or *i*) and *z* are pronounced like the *th* in "thin"; in the south of Spain and in *all* Spanish America like the *s* in "see". In Spain

---

[1] In Mexico the depreciative word for a Spaniard is *gachupín, –a.*

the *th* value is considered more correct, although the *s* value is honored as an admissible alternative when coming from southern Spaniards and Spanish Americans. However, a northern Spaniard who employed the *s* value would be considered uncultured by his countrymen.

In Spanish America the *s* value is the only natural sound.

> NOTE: Do not be surprised if you find that with many Spanish Americans *s* (and *z)* before a consonant and at the end of a word is changed to Spanish *j* (like *h* in *"hat")*: *ujté* (usted), *conojco* (conozco), *hajta* (hasta), *lo jotroj* (los otros). This occurs in the coastal regions of South America, throughout the Antilles, and in the south of Spain. While this trait is fairly widespread, you had better not imitate it. Some speakers will drop the *s* and *z* entirely; this is even less desirable.

ll, y Here the situation is somewhat different from that of *c, z,* and *s*. In Spain the great majority of speakers pronounce *ll* as the *ly* sound heard in "billiard". In Spanish America most people pronounce it as *y*, although there are areas (the interior of Colombia, Ecuador, Peru, parts of Paraguay and Bolivia) where the Castilian *ly* sound is quite natural. In Spain, the *y* sound is found in the south and is frequently associated with the lower classes.

The *ly* pronunciation in both Spain and Spanish America is considered culturally more important than the *th* sound for *c* and *z*. Thus you will find that even those Spanish Americans who normally pronounce *ll* as *y*, will sometimes change to the *ly* sound in highly ceremonious and elevated speech. On the other hand, the Castilian *th* sound is never used by native Spanish Americans.

For Spanish American purposes, you are advised to adopt the *y* sound, since this is by far the most natural and frequent pronunciation.

NOTE: You will find that Cubans, Puerto Ricans, Dominicans, certain Central Americans (Salvadorians and Costa Ricans), and many South Americans frequently pronounce *ll* and *y* something like the *j* in "Joe". Among the coastal Argentines and Uruguayans, the sound is that of the *s* in "pleasure". Both variants are heard in the south of Spain.

APPENDIX

THE use of the material in this section is self-explanatory. The purpose is to clarify certain dubious points and confusions by presenting in juxtaposition a number of similarities and differences in meaning and appearance.

Words with Two Genders

el capital = the capital (money)	*la capital* = the capital (city)
el corte = the cut	*la corte* = the court
el policía = the policeman	*la policía* = the police (force)
el cura = the priest	*la cura* = the cure
el frente = the front	*la frente* = the forehead

For remarks on *orden*, see ORDER in Part II.

Do Not Confuse

el banco = the bank, bench	*la banca* = the banking
el fruto = the fruit (on a tree)	*la fruta* = edible fruit
el pago = the payment	*la paga* = the pay
el grito = the cry, shout	*la grita* = the shouting
el madero = the board	*la madera* = the wood
el leño = the piece of timber	*la leña* = the timber
el pato = the duck	*la pata* = the foot (of an animal)
el puerto = the port, harbor	*la puerta* = the door
el naranjo[1] = the orange tree	*la naranja* = the orange

[1] With regard to fruits, note that the tree is usually masculine and the fruit is feminine: *cerezo* = cherry tree; *cereza* = cherry.

Words of Multiple Function

Confusion often results from the same word entering into several idioms. Study the following and note the differences in meaning.

DÍA

de día = by day, in the daytime
del día = of the present day
al día = per day, by the day
hoy (en) día = nowadays
hoy por hoy = this very day
el otro día = the other day
al otro día = on the next day

LADO

a un lado = aside
al lado = to one side
al lado de = at the side of
de lado = sidewise
por otro lado = on the other hand

PRONTO

de pronto = suddenly
al pronto = at first
por de pronto = for the time being

PASO

a cada paso = at every step
paso a paso = step by step
al paso = in passing
de paso = in passing
al paso que = while, as
dar un paso = to take a step

FIN

a fines de = at the end of
a fin de = in order to
por fin = at last
al fin = finally
en fin = all in all, after all
al fin y al cabo = finally

CONTRARIO

al contrario = on the contrary
de lo contrario = otherwise
por el contrario = otherwise

92

TODO

sobre todo = especially
ante todo = first of all
del todo = entirely
con todo = nevertheless
a todo = at most

CASO

en último caso = as a last resort
en todo caso = in any case
en tal caso = in such a case

OCUPARSE

ocuparse de = to attend to
ocuparse con = to busy one's self with
ocuparse en = to be engaged in

VEZ

a la vez = at a time, at the same time
de una vez = once and for all
en vez de = instead of
tal vez = perhaps
de vez en cuando = from time to time
alguna vez = ever
algunas veces = sometimes
a veces = at times
otra vez = again
otras veces = on other occasions
muchas veces = many times
varias veces = several times
pocas veces = seldom
rara vez = seldom
a la vez que = while
toda vez que = whenever

ACABAR

acabar = to finish, complete
acabar con = to put an end to, destroy, get rid of
acabar (in preterite) de + *infinitive* = to finish (doing something)
acabar (in present or imperfect) de + *infinitive* = to have just (done something)

Multiple Translations

Many of the following idioms are easily confused because their meanings are not always obvious.

as soon as	*as soon as possible*	*although*
en cuanto	cuanto antes	aunque
tan pronto como	lo más pronto posible	si bien
luego que	tan pronto posible	bien que
así que	lo antes posible	

in regard to	*at least*	*at most*
en cuanto a	por lo menos	a lo más
con respecto a	al menos	cuando más
respecto a (de)	cuando menos	a todo
tocante a	a lo menos	por lo más
		a lo sumo

suddenly	*nevertheless*	*on the other hand*
de pronto	sin embargo	en cambio
de repente	no obstante	por otra parte
de golpe	con todo	por otro lado
de súbito		

at once	*certainly*	*to bear in mind, realize*
al momento	desde luego	darse cuenta de
al instante	seguramente	tener en cuenta
en seguida[1]	de seguro	tener presente
en el acto	ciertamente	hacerse cargo de
al punto	por cierto	
inmediatamente	claro	
desde luego	por supuesto	

---

[1] In the Argentine *en seguida* means the opposite, *i.e.* "presently", "later".